THE OVERCOMING LIFE

AND OTHER SERMONS

The Hard Hitting Christian Classic From the Greatest
Evangelist Of The 19th Century.

By D. L. MOODY.

"This is the victory that overcometh the world, even our
faith."

Originally published in 1896.

CONTENTS.

PART I.

THE CHRISTIAN'S WARFARE.

I would like to have you open your Bible at the first epistle of John, fifth chapter, fourth and fifth verses: "Whatsoever is born of God overcometh the world: and this is the victory that overcometh the world, even our faith. Who is he that overcometh the world, but he that believeth that Jesus is the Son of God?"

When a battle is fought, all are anxious to know who are the victors. In these verses we are told who is to gain the victory in life. When I was converted I made this mistake: I thought the battle was already mine, the victory already won, the crown already in my grasp. I thought that old things had passed away, that all things had become new; that my old corrupt nature, the Adam life, was gone. But I found out, after serving Christ for a few months, that conversion was only like enlisting in the army, that there was a battle on hand, and that if I was to get a crown, I had to work for it and fight for it.

Salvation is a gift, as free as the air we breathe. It is to be obtained, like any other gift, without money and without price: there are no other terms. "To him that worketh not, but believeth." But on the other hand, if we are to gain a crown, we must work for it. Let me quote a few verses in First Corinthians: "For other foundation can no man lay than that which is laid, which is Jesus Christ. But if any man buildeth on the foundation gold, silver, costly stones, wood, hay, stubble; each man's work shall be made manifest: for the day shall declare it, because it is revealed in fire: and the fire itself shall prove each man's work, of what sort it is. If any man's work shall abide, which he built thereon, he shall receive a reward. If any man's work shall be burned, he shall suffer loss: but he himself shall be saved; yet so as through fire."

We see clearly from this that we may be saved, but all our works burned up. I may have a wretched, miserable voyage through life, with no victory, and no reward at the end; saved, yet so as by fire, or as Job puts it, "with the skin of my teeth." I believe that a great many men will barely get to heaven as Lot got out of Sodom, burned out, nothing left, works and everything else destroyed.

It is like this: when a man enters the army, he is a member of the army the moment he enlists; he is just as much a member as a man who has been in the army ten or twenty years. But enlisting is one thing, and participating in a battle another. Young converts are like those just enlisted.

It is folly for any man to attempt to fight in his own strength. The world, the flesh and the devil are too much for any man. But if we are linked to Christ by faith, and He is formed in us the hope of glory, then we shall get the victory over every enemy. It is believers who are the overcomers. "Thanks be unto God, which always causeth us to triumph in Christ." Through Him we shall be more than conquerors.

I wouldn't think of talking to unconverted men about overcoming the world, for it is utterly impossible. They might as well try to cut down the American forest with their penknives. But a good many Christian people make this mistake: they think the battle is already fought and won. They have an idea that all they have to do is to put the oars down in the bottom of the boat, and the current will drift them into the ocean of God's eternal love. But we have to cross the current. We have to learn how to watch and fight, and how to overcome. The battle is only just commenced. The Christian life is a conflict and a warfare, and the quicker we find it out the better. There is not a blessing in this world that God has not linked Himself to. All the great and higher blessings God associates with Himself. When God and man work together, then it is that there is going to be victory. We are coworkers with Him. You might take a mill, and put it forty feet above a river, and there isn't capital enough in the States to make that river turn the mill; but get it down about forty feet, and away it works. We want to keep in mind that if we are going to overcome the world, we have got to work with God. It is His power that makes all the means of grace effectual.

The story is told that Frederick Douglas, the great slave orator, once said in a mournful speech when things looked dark for his race:—

"The white man is against us, governments are against us, the spirit of the times is against us. I see no hope for the colored race. I am full of sadness."

Just then a poor old colored woman rose in the audience, and said.—

"Frederick, is God dead?"

My friend, it makes a difference when you count God in.

Now many a young believer is discouraged and disheartened when he realizes this warfare. He begins to think that God has forsaken him, that Christianity is not all that it professes to be. But he should rather regard it as an encouraging sign. No sooner has a soul escaped from his snare than the great Adversary takes steps to ensnare it again. He puts forth all his power to recapture his lost prey. The fiercest attacks are made on the strongest forts, and the fiercer the battle the young believer is called on to wage, the surer evidence it is of the work of the Holy Spirit in his heart. God will not desert him in his time of need, any more than He deserted His people of old when they were hard pressed by their foes.

The Only Complete Victor.

This brings me to the fourth verse of the fourth chapter of the same epistle: "Ye are of God, little children, and have overcome them: because greater is He that is in you than he that is in the world." The only man that ever conquered this world—was complete victor—was Jesus Christ. When He shouted on the cross, "It is finished!" it was the shout of a conqueror. He had overcome every enemy. He had met sin and death. He had met every foe that you and I have got to meet, and had come off victor. Now if I have got the spirit of Christ, if I have got that same life in me, then it is that I have got a power that is greater than any power in the world, and with that same power I overcome the world.

Notice that everything human in this world fails. Every man, the moment he takes his eye off God, has failed. Every man has been a failure at some period of his life. Abraham failed. Moses failed. Elijah failed. Take the men that have become so famous and that were so mighty—the moment they got their eye off God, they were weak like other men; and it is a very singular thing that those men failed on the strongest point in their character. I suppose it was because they were not on the watch. Abraham was noted for his faith, and he failed right there—he denied his wife. Moses was noted for his meekness and humility, and he failed right there—he got angry. God kept him out of the promised land because he lost his temper. I know he was called "the servant of God," and that he was a mighty man, and had power with God, but humanly speaking, he failed, and was kept out of the promised land. Elijah was noted for his power in prayer and for his courage, yet he became a coward. He was the boldest man of his day, and stood before Ahab, and the royal court, and all the prophets of Baal; yet when he heard that Jezebel had threatened his life, he ran away to the desert, and under a juniper tree prayed that he might die. Peter was noted for his boldness, and a little maid scared him nearly out of his wits. As soon as she spoke to him, he began to tremble, and he swore that he didn't know Christ. I have often said to myself that I'd like to have been there on the day of Pentecost alongside of that maid when she saw Peter preaching.

"Why," I suppose she said, "what has come over that man? He was afraid of me only a few weeks ago, and now he stands up before all Jerusalem and charges these very Jews with the murder of Jesus."

The moment he got his eye off the Master he failed; and every man, I don't care who he is—even the strongest—every man that hasn't Christ in him, is a failure. John, the beloved disciple, was noted for his meekness; and yet we hear of him wanting to call fire down from heaven on a little town because it had refused the common hospitalities.

Triumphs of Faith.

Now, how are we to get the victory over all our enemies? Turn to Galatians, second chapter, verse twenty: "I am crucified with Christ; nevertheless I live; yet not I, but Christ liveth in me: and the life which I now live in the flesh, I live by the faith of the Son of God, who loved me and gave Himself for me." We live by faith. We get this life by faith, and become linked to Immanuel—"God with us." If I have God for me, I am going to overcome. How do we gain this mighty power? By faith.

The next passage I want to call your attention to is Romans, chapter eleven, verse twenty: "Because of unbelief they were broken off; and thou standest by faith." The Jews were cut off on account of their unbelief: we were grafted in on account of our belief. So notice: We live by faith, and we stand by faith.

Next: We walk by faith. Second Corinthians, chapter five, verse seven: "For we walk by faith, not by sight." The most faulty Christians I know are those who want to walk by sight. They want to see the end—how a thing is going to come out. That isn't walking by faith at all—that is walking by sight.

I think the characters that best represent this difference are Joseph and Jacob. Jacob was a man who walked with God by sight. You remember his vow at Bethel:—"If God will be with me, and will keep me in this way that I go, and will give me bread to eat, and raiment to put on, so that I come again to my father's house in peace; then shall the Lord be my God." And you remember how his heart revived when he saw the wagons Joseph sent him from Egypt. He sought after signs. He never could have gone through the temptations and trials that his son Joseph did. Joseph represents a higher type of Christian. He could walk in the dark. He could survive thirteen years of misfortune, in spite of his dreams, and then ascribe it all to the goodness and providence of God.

Lot and Abraham are a good illustration Lot turned away from Abraham and tented on the plains of Sodom. He got a good stretch of pasture land, but he had bad neighbors. He was a weak character and he should have kept with Abraham in order to get strong. A good many men are just like that. As long as their mothers are living, or they are bolstered up by some godly person, they get along very well; but they can't stand alone. Lot walked by sight; but Abraham walked by faith; he went out in the footsteps of God. "By faith Abraham, when he was called to go out into a place which he should after receive for an inheritance, obeyed; and he went out, not knowing whither he went. By faith he sojourned in the land of promise, as in a strange country, dwelling in tabernacles with Isaac and Jacob, the heirs with him of the same promise: for he looked for a city which hath foundations, whose builder and maker is God." And again: We fight by faith. Ephesians, sixth chapter, verse sixteen: "Above all, taking the shield of faith, wherewith ye shall be able to quench all the fiery darts of the wicked." Every dart Satan can fire at us we can quench by faith, By faith we can overcome the Evil One. To fear is to have more faith in your antagonist than in Christ.

Some of the older people can remember when our war broke out. Secretary Seward, who was Lincoln's Secretary of State—a long-headed and shrewd politician— prophesied that the war would be over in ninety days; and young men in thousands and hundreds of thousands came forward and volunteered to go down to Dixie and whip the South. They thought they would be back in ninety days; but the war lasted four years, and cost about half a million of lives. What was the matter? Why, the South was a good deal stronger than the North supposed. Its strength was underestimated.

Jesus Christ makes no mistake of that kind. When He enlists a man in His service, He shows him the dark side; He lets him know that he must live a life of self-denial. If a man is not willing to go to heaven by the way of Calvary, he cannot go at all. Many men want a religion in which there is no cross, but they cannot enter heaven that way. If we are to be disciples of Jesus Christ, we must deny ourselves and take up our cross and follow Him. So let us sit down and count the cost. Do not think that you will have no battles if you follow the Nazarene, because many battles are before you. Yet if I had ten thousand lives, Jesus Christ should have every one of them. Men do not object to a battle if they are confident that they will have victory, and, thank God, every one of us may have the victory if we will.

The reason why so many Christians fail all through life is just this—they under-estimate the strength of the enemy. My dear friend; you and I have got a terrible enemy to contend with. Don't let Satan deceive you. Unless you are spiritually dead, it means warfare. Nearly everything around tends to draw us away from God. We do not step clear out of Egypt on to the throne of God. There is the wilderness journey, and there are enemies in the land.

Don't let any man or woman think all he or she has to do is to join the church. That will not save you. The question is, are you overcoming the world, or is the world overcoming you? Are you more patient than you were five years ago?

Are you more amiable? If you are not, the world is overcoming you, even if you are a church member. That epistle that Paul wrote to Titus says that we are to be sound in patience, faith and charity. We have got Christians, a good many of them, that are good in spots, but mighty poor in other spots. Just a little bit of them seems to be saved, you know. They are not rounded out in their characters. It is just because they haven't been taught that they have a terrible foe to overcome.

If I wanted to find out whether a Man was a Christian, I wouldn't go to his minister. I would go and ask his wife. I tell you, we want more home piety just now. If a man doesn't treat his wife right, I don't want to hear him talk about Christianity. What is the use of his talking about salvation for the next life, if he has no salvation for this? We want a Christianity that goes into our homes and everyday lives. Some men's religion just repels me. They put on a whining voice and a sort of a religious tone, and talk so sanctimoniously on Sunday that you would think they were wonderful saints. But on Monday they are quite different. They put their religion away with their clothes, and you don't see any more of it until the next Sunday. You laugh, but let us look out that we don't belong to that class. My friend, we have got to have a higher type of Christianity, or the Church is gone. It is wrong for a man or woman to profess what they don't possess. If you are not overcoming temptations, the world is overcoming you. Just get on your knees and ask God to help you. My dear friends, let us go to God and ask Him to search us. Let us ask Him to wake us up, and let us not think that just because we are church members we are all right. We are all wrong if we are not getting victory over sin.

PART II.

INTERNAL FOES.

Now if we are going to overcome, we must begin inside.
God always begins there. An enemy inside the fort is far
more dangerous than one outside.

Scripture teaches that in every believer there are two
natures warring against each other. Paul says in his epistle
to the Romans:—"For we know that the law is spiritual: but
I am carnal, sold under sin. For that which I do I allow not:
for what I would, that do I not; but what I hate, that do I. If
then I do that which I would not, I consent unto the law that
it is good. Now then it is no more I that do it, but sin that
dwelleth in me. For I know that in me (that is, in my flesh,)
dwelleth no good thing: for to will is present with me; but
how to perform that which is good I find not. For the good
that I would I do not: but the evil which I would not, that I
do. Now if I do that I would not, it is no more I that do it,
but sin that dwelleth in me. I find then a law, that when I
would do good, evil is present with me. For I delight in the
law of God after the inward man: but I see another law in
my members, warring against the law of my mind, and
bringing me into captivity to the law of sin which is in my
members." Again, in the Epistle to the Galatians, he says:
"For the flesh lusteth against the Spirit, and the Spirit
against the flesh: and these are contrary the one to the
other: so that ye cannot do the things that ye would."

When we are born of God, we get His nature, but He does
not immediately take away all the old nature. Each species

of animal and bird is true to its nature. You can tell the nature of the dove or canary bird. The horse is true to his nature, the cow is true to hers. But a man has two natures, and do not let the world or Satan make you think that the old nature is extinct, because it is not. "Reckon ye yourselves dead"; but if you were dead, you wouldn't need to reckon yourselves dead, would you? The dead self would be dropped out of the reckoning. "I keep my body under"; if it were dead, Paul wouldn't have needed to keep it under. I am judicially dead, but the old nature is alive, and therefore if I don't keep my body under and crucify the flesh with its affections, this lower nature will gain the advantage, and I shall be in bondage. Many men live all their lives in bondage to the old nature, when they might have liberty if they would only live this overcoming life. The old Adam never dies. It remains corrupt. "From the sole of the foot even unto the head there is no soundness in it; but wounds, and bruises, and putrifying sores: they have not been closed, neither bound up, neither mollified with ointment."

A gentleman in India once got a tiger-cub, and tamed it so that it became a pet. One day when it had grown up, it tasted blood, and the old tiger-nature flashed out, and it had to be killed. So with the old nature in the believer. It never dies, though it is subdued: and unless he is watchful and prayerful, it will gain the upper hand, and rush him into sin. Someone has pointed out that "I" is the centre of S-I-N. It is the medium through which Satan acts.

And so the worst enemy you have to overcome, after all, is yourself. When Capt. T— became converted in London, he was a great society man. After he had been a Christian some months, he was asked;

"What have you found to be your greatest enemy since you began to be a Christian?"

After a few minutes of deep thought he said, "Well, I think it is myself."

"Ah!" said the lady, "the King has taken you into His presence, for it is only in His presence that we are taught these truths."

I have had more trouble with D. L. Moody than with any other man who has crossed my path. If I can only keep him right, I don't have any trouble with other people. A good many have trouble with servants. Did you ever think that the trouble lies with you instead of the servants? If one member of the family is constantly snapping, he will have the whole family snapping. It is true whether you believe it or not. You speak quickly and snappishly to people and they will do the same to you.

Appetite.

Now take appetite. That is an enemy inside. How many young men are ruined by the appetite for strong drink! Many a young man has grown up to be a curse to his father and mother, instead of a blessing. Not long ago the body of a young suicide was discovered in one of our large cities. In his pocket was found a paper on which he had written: "I have done this myself. Don't tell anyone. It is all through drink." An intimation of these facts in the public press drew two hundred and forty six letters from two hundred and forty six families, each of whom had a prodigal son who, it was feared, might be the suicide.

Strong drink is an enemy, both to body and soul. It is reported that Sir Andrew Clarke, the celebrated London physician, once made the following statement: "Now let me say that I am speaking solemnly and carefully when I tell you that I am considerably within the mark in saying that within the rounds of my hospital wards today, seven out of every ten that lie there in their beds owe their ill health to alcohol. I do not say that seventy in every hundred are drunkards; I do not know that one of them is; but they use alcohol. So soon as a man begins to take one drop, then the desire begotten in him becomes a part of his nature, and that nature, formed by his acts, inflicts curses inexpressible when handed down to the generations that are to follow him as part and parcel of their being. When I think of this I am disposed to give up my profession—to give up everything—and to go forth upon a holy crusade to preach to all men, 'Beware of this enemy of the race!'"

It is the most destructive agency in the world today. It kills more than the bloodiest wars. It is the fruitful parent of crime and idleness and poverty and disease. It spoils a man for this world, and damns him for the next. The Word of God has declared it: "Be not deceived: neither fornicators, nor idolaters, nor adulterers, . . . nor drunkards . . . shall inherit the Kingdom of God."

How can we overcome this enemy? Bitter experience proves that man is not powerful enough in his own strength. The only cure for the accursed appetite is regeneration—a new life—the power of the risen Christ within us. Let a man that is given to strong drink look to God for help, and He will give him victory over his appetite. Jesus Christ came to destroy the works of the devil, and He will take away that appetite if you will let Him.

Temper.

Then there is temper. I wouldn't give much for a man that hasn't temper. Steel isn't good for anything if it hasn't got temper. But when temper gets the mastery over me I am its slave, and it is a source of weakness. It may be made a great power for good all through my life, and help me; or it may become my greatest enemy from within, and rob me of power. The current in some rivers is so strong as to make them useless for navigation.

Someone has said that a preacher will never miss the people when he speaks of temper. It is astonishing how little mastery even professing Christians have over it. A friend of mine in England was out visiting, and while sitting in the parlor, heard an awful noise in the hall. He asked what it meant, and was told that it was only the doctor throwing his boots downstairs because they were not properly blacked. "Many Christians," said an old divine, "who bore the loss of a child or of all their property with the most heroic Christian fortitude, are entirely vanquished by the breaking of a dish or the blunders of a servant."

I have had people say to me, "Mr. Moody, how can I get control of my temper?"

If you really want to get control, I will tell you how, but you won't like the medicine. Treat it as a sin and confess it. People look upon it as a sort of a misfortune, and one lady told me she inherited it from her father and mother. Supposing she did. That is no excuse for her.

When you get angry again and speak unkindly to a person, and when you realize it, go and ask that person to forgive you. You won't get mad with that person for the next twenty-four hours. You might do it in about forty eight hours, but go the second time, and after you have done it about half-a-dozen times, you will get out of the business, because it makes the old flesh burn.

A lady said to me once, "I have got so in the habit of exaggerating that my friends accuse me of exaggerating so that they don't understand me."

She said, "Can you help me? What can I do to overcome it?"

"Well," I said, "the next time you catch yourself lying, go right to that party and say you have lied, and tell him you are sorry. Say it is a lie; stamp it out, root and branch; that is what you want to do."

"Oh," she said, "I wouldn't like to call it lying." But that is what it was.

Christianity isn't worth a snap of your finger if it doesn't straighten out your character. I have got tired of all mere gush and sentiment. If people can't tell when you are telling the truth, there is something radically wrong, and you had better straighten it out right away. Now, are you ready to do it? Bring yourself to it whether you want to or not. Do you find someone who has been offended by something you have done? Go right to them and tell them you are sorry. You say you are not to blame. Never mind, go right to them, and tell them you are sorry. I have had to do it a good many times. An impulsive man like myself has to do it often, but I sleep all the sweeter at night when I get things straightened out. Confession never fails to bring a blessing. I have sometimes had to get off the platform and go down and ask a man's forgiveness before I could go on preaching. A Christian man ought to be a gentleman every time; but if he is not, and he finds he has wounded or hurt someone, he ought to go and straighten it out at once. You know there are a great many people who want just Christianity enough to make them respectable. They don't think about this overcoming life that gets the victory all the time. They have their blue days and their cross days, and the children say,

"Mother is cross to-day, and you will have to be very careful."

We don't want any of these touchy blue days; these ups and downs. If we are overcoming, that is the effect our life is going to have on others, they will have confidence in our Christianity. The reason that many a man has no power, is that there is some cursed sin covered up. There will not be a drop of dew until that sin is brought to light. Get right inside. Then we can go out like giants and conquer the world if everything is right within.

Paul says that we are to be sound in faith, in patience, and in love. If a man is unsound in his faith, the clergy take the ecclesiastical sword and cut him off at once. But he may be ever so unsound in charity, in patience, and nothing is said about that. We must be sound in faith, in love, and in patience if we are to be true to God.

How delightful it is to meet a man who can control his temper! It is said of Wilberforce that a friend once found him in the greatest agitation, looking for a dispatch he had mislaid, for which one of the royal family was waiting. Just then, as if to make it still more trying, a disturbance was heard in the nursery.

"Now," thought the friend, "surely his temper will give way."

The thought had hardly passed through his mind when Wilberforce turned to him and said:

"What a blessing it is to hear those dear children! Only think what a relief, among other hurries, to hear their voices and know they are well."

Covetousness.

Take the sin of covetousness. There is more said in the Bible against it than against drunkenness. I must get it out of me—destroy it, root and branch—and not let it have dominion over me. We think that a man who gets drunk is a horrid monster, but a covetous man will often be received into the church, and put into office, who is as vile and black in the sight of God as any drunkard.

The most dangerous thing about this sin is that it is not generally regarded as very heinous. Of course we all have a contempt for misers, but all covetous men are not misers. Another thing to be noted about it is that it fastens upon the old rather than upon the young.

Let us see what the Bible says about covetousness:—

"Mortify therefore your members . . . covetousness, which is idolatry."

"No covetous man hath any inheritance in the Kingdom of God."

"They that will be (that is, desire to be) rich fall into temptation and a snare, and into many foolish and hurtful lusts, which drown men in destruction and perdition.

For the love of money is the root of all evil: which while some coveted after, they have erred from the faith, and pierced themselves through with many sorrows."

"The wicked blesseth the covetous, whom the Lord abhorreth."

Covetousness enticed Lot into Sodom. It caused the destruction of Achan and all his house. It was the iniquity of Balaam. It was the sin of Samuel's sons. It left Gehazi a leper. It sent the rich young ruler away sorrowful. It led Judas to sell his Master and Lord. It brought about the death of Ananias and Sapphira. It was the blot in the character of Felix. What victims it has had in all ages!

Do you say: "How am I going to check covetousness?"

Well,—I don't think there is any difficulty about that. If you find yourself getting very covetous—very miserly— wanting to get everything you can into your possession— just begin to scatter. Just say to covetousness that you will strangle it, and rid it out of your disposition.

A wealthy farmer in New York state, who had been a noted miser, a very selfish man, was converted. Soon after his conversion a poor man came to him one day to ask for help. He had been burned out, and had no provisions. This young convert thought he would be liberal and give him a ham from his smoke house. He started toward the smoke-house, and on the way the tempter said,

"Give him the smallest one you have."

He struggled all the way as to whether he would give a large or a small one. In order to overcome his selfishness, he took down the biggest ham and gave it to the man.

The tempter said, "You are a fool."

But he replied, "If you don't keep still, I will give him every ham I have in the smoke-house."

If you find that you are selfish, give something. Determine to overcome that spirit of selfishness, and to keep your body under, no matter what it may cost.

Mr. Durant told me he was engaged by Goodyear to defend the rubber patent, and he was to have half of the money that came from the patent, if he succeeded. One day he woke up to find that he was a rich man, and he said that the greatest struggle of his life then took place as to whether he would let money be his master, or he be master of money, whether he would be its slave, or make it a slave to him. At last he got the victory, and that is how Wellesley College was built.

Are You Jealous, Envious?

Go and do a good turn for that person of whom you are jealous. That is the way to cure jealousy; it will kill it. Jealousy is a devil, it is a horrid monster. The poets imagined that Envy dwelt in a dark cave, being pale and thin, looking asquint, never rejoicing except in the misfortune of others, and hurting himself continually.

There is a fable of an eagle which could outfly another, and the other didn't like it. The latter saw a sportsman one day, and said to him,

"I wish you would bring down that eagle."

The sportsman replied that he would if he only had some feathers to put into the arrow. So the eagle pulled one out of his wing. The arrow was shot, but didn't quite reach the rival eagle; it was flying too high. The envious eagle pulled out more feathers, and kept pulling them out until he lost so many that he couldn't fly, and then the sportsman turned around and killed him. My friend, if you are jealous, the only man you can hurt is yourself.

There were two business men—merchants—and there was great rivalry between them, a great deal of bitter feeling. One of them was converted. He went to his minister and said,

"I am still jealous of that man, and I do not know how to overcome it."

"Well," he said, "if a man comes into your store to buy goods, and you cannot supply him, just send him over to your neighbor."

He said he wouldn't like to do that.

"Well," the minister said, "you do it and you will kill jealousy."

He said he would, and when a customer came into his store for goods which he did not have, he would tell him to go across the street to his neighbor's. By and by the other began to send his customers over to this man's store, and the breach was healed.

Pride.

Then there is pride. This is another of those sins which the Bible so strongly condemns, but which the world hardly reckons as a sin at all. "An high look and a proud heart is sin." "Everyone that is proud in heart is an abomination to the Lord; though hand join in hand, he shall not be unpunished." Christ included pride among those evil things which, proceeding out of the heart of a man, defile him.

People have an idea that it is just the wealthy who are proud. But go down on some of the back streets, and you will find that some of the very poorest are as proud as the richest. It is the heart, you know. People that haven't any money are just as proud as those that have. We have got to crush it out. It is an enemy. You needn't be proud of your face, for there is not one but that after ten days in the grave the worms would be eating your body. There is nothing to be proud of—is there? Let us ask God to deliver us from pride.

You can't fold your arms and say, "Lord, take it out of me"; but just go and work with Him.

Mortify your pride by cultivating humility. "Put on, therefore," says Paul, "as the elect of God, holy and beloved, . . . humbleness of mind." "Be clothed with humility," says Peter. "Blessed are the poor in spirit."

PART III.

EXTERNAL FOES.

What are our enemies without? What does James say? "Know ye not that the friendship of the world is enmity with God? whosoever therefore will be a friend of the world is the enemy of God." And John? "Love not the world, neither the things that are in the world. If any man love the world, the love of the Father is not in him."

Now, people want to know what is the world. When you talk with them they say:

"Well, when you say 'the world,' what do you mean?"

Here we have the answer in the next verse: "For all that is in the world, the lust of the flesh, and the lust of the eyes, and the pride of life, is not of the Father, but is of the world. And the world passeth away, and the lust thereof: but he that doeth the will of God abideth forever."

"The world" does not mean nature around us. God nowhere tells us that the material world is an enemy to be overcome. On the contrary, we read: "The earth is the Lord's, and the fulness thereof; the world, and they that dwell therein." "The heavens declare the glory of God; and the firmament sheweth His handywork."

It means "human life and society as far as alienated from God, through being centered on material aims and objects, and thus opposed to God's Spirit and kingdom." Christ said: "If the world hate you, ye know that it hated Me before it hated you . . . the world hath hated them because they are not of the world, even as I am not of the world." Love of the world means the forgetfulness of the eternal future by reason of love for passing things.

How can the world be overcome? Not by education, not by experience; only by faith. "This is the victory that overcometh the world, even our faith. Who is he that overcometh the world, but he that believeth that Jesus is the Son of God?"

Worldly Habits and Fashions.

For one thing we must fight worldly habits and fashions. We must often go against the customs of the world. I have great respect for a man who can stand up for what he believes is right against all the world. He who can stand alone is a hero.

Suppose it is the custom for young men to do certain things you wouldn't like your mother to know of—things that your mother taught you are wrong. You may have to stand up alone among all your companions.

They will say: "You can't get away from your mother, eh? Tied to your mother's apron strings!"

But just you say: "Yes! I have some respect for my mother. She taught me what is right, and she is the best friend I have. I believe that is wrong, and I am going to stand for the right." If you have to stand alone, stand. Enoch did it, and Joseph, and Elisha, and Paul. God has kept such men in all ages.

Someone says: "I move in society where they have wine parties. I know it is rather a dangerous thing because my son is apt to follow me. But I can stop just where I want to; perhaps my son hasn't got the same power as I have, and he may go over the dam. But it is the custom in the society where I move."

Once I got into a place where I had to get up and leave. I was invited into a home, and they had a late supper, and there were seven kinds of liquor on the table. I am ashamed to say they were Christian people. A deacon urged a young lady to drink until her face flushed. I rose from the table and went out; I felt that it was no place for me. They considered me very rude. That was going against custom; that was entering a protest against such an infernal thing. Let us go against custom, when it leads astray.

I was told in a southern college, some years ago, that no man was considered a first class gentleman who did not drink. Of course it is not so now.

Pleasure.

Another enemy is worldly pleasure. A great many people are just drowned in pleasure. They have no time for any meditation at all. Many a man has been lost to society, and lost to his family, by giving himself up to the god of pleasure. God wants His children to be happy, but in a way that will help and not hinder them.

A lady came to me once and said: "Mr. Moody, I wish you would tell me how I can become a Christian." The tears were rolling down her cheeks, and she was in a very favorable mood; "but," she said, "I don't want to be one of your kind."

"Well," I asked, "have I got any peculiar kind? What is the matter with my Christianity?"

"Well," she said, "my father was a doctor, and had a large practice, and he used to get so tired that he used to take us to the theater. There was a large family of girls, and we had tickets for the theaters three or four times a week. I suppose we were there a good deal oftener than we were in church. I am married to a lawyer, and he has a large practice. He gets so tired that he takes us out to the theater," and she said, "I am far better acquainted with the theater and theater people than with the church and church people, and I don't want to give up the theater."

"Well," I said, "did you ever hear me say anything about theaters? There have been reporters here every day for all the different papers, and they are giving my sermons verbatim in one paper. Have you ever seen anything in the sermons against the theaters?"

She said, "No."

"Well," I said, "I have seen you in the audience every afternoon for several weeks and have you heard me say anything against theaters?"

No, she hadn't.

"Well," I said, "what made you bring them up?" "Why, I supposed you didn't believe in theaters." "What made you think that?"

"Why," she said, "Do you ever go?"

"No."

"Why don't you go?"

"Because I have got something better. I would sooner go out into the street and eat dirt than do some of the things I used to do before I became a Christian."

"Why!" she said, "I don't understand."

"Never mind," I said. "When Jesus Christ has the pre-eminence, you will understand it all. He didn't come down here and say we shouldn't go here and we shouldn't go there, and lay down a lot of rules; but He laid down great principles. Now, He says if you love Him you will take delight in pleasing Him." And I began to preach Christ to her. The tears started again. She said:

"I tell you, Mr. Moody, that sermon on the indwelling Christ yesterday afternoon just broke my heart. I admire Him, and I want to be a Christian, but I don't want to give up the theaters."

I said, "Please don't mention them again. I don't want to talk about theaters. I want to talk to you about Christ." So I took my Bible, and I read to her about Christ.

But she said again, "Mr. Moody, can I go to the theater if I become a Christian?"

"Yes," I said, "you can go to the theater just as much as you like if you are a real, true Christian, and can go with His blessing."

"Well," she said, "I am glad you are not so narrow-minded as some."

She felt quite relieved to think that she could go to the theaters and be a Christian. But I said,

"If you can go to the theater for the glory of God, keep on going; only be sure that you go for the glory of God. If you are a Christian you will be glad to do whatever will please Him."

I really think she became a Christian that day. The burden had gone, there was joy; but just as she was leaving me at the door, she said,

"I am not going to give up the theater."

In a few days she came back to me and said, "Mr. Moody, I understand all about that theater business now. I went the other night. There was a large party at our house, and my husband wanted us to go, and we went; but when the curtain lifted, everything looked so different. I said to my husband, 'This is no place for me; this is horrible. I am not going to stay here, I am going home.' He said, 'Don't make a fool of yourself. Everyone has heard that you have been converted in the Moody meetings, and if you go out, it will be all through fashionable society, I beg of you don't make a fool of yourself by getting up and going out.' But I said, 'I have been making a fool of myself all of my life.'"

Now, the theater hadn't changed, but she had got something better and she was going to overcome the world. "They that are after the flesh do mind the things of the flesh; but they that are after the Spirit the things of the Spirit." When Christ has the first place in your heart you are going to get victory. Just do whatever you know will please Him. The great objection I have to these things is that they get the mastery, and become a hindrance to spiritual growth.

Business.

It may be that we have got to overcome in business. Perhaps it is business morning, noon and night, and Sundays, too. When a man will drive like Jehu all the week and like a snail on Sunday, isn't there something wrong with him? Now, business is legitimate; and a man is not, I think, a good citizen that will not go out and earn his bread by the sweat of his brow; and he ought to be a good business man, and whatever he does, do thoroughly. At the same time, if he lays his whole heart on his business, and makes a god of it, and thinks more of it than anything else, then the world has come in. It may be very legitimate in its place—like fire, which, in its place, is one of the best friends of man; out of place, is one of the worst enemies of man;—like water, which we cannot live without; and yet, when not in place, it becomes an enemy.

So my friends, that is the question for you and me to settle. Now look at yourself. Are you getting the victory? Are you growing more even in your disposition? are you getting mastery over the world and the flesh?

And bear this in mind: Every temptation you overcome makes you stronger to overcome others, while every temptation that defeats you makes you weaker. You can become weaker and weaker, or you can become stronger and stronger. Sin takes the pith out of your sinews, but virtue makes you stronger. How many men have been overcome by some little thing! Turn a moment to the Song of Solomon, the second chapter, fifteenth verse: "Take us the foxes, the little foxes that spoil the vines: for our vines have tender grapes." A great many people seem to think these little things—getting out of patience, using little deceits, telling white lies (as they call them), and when somebody calls on you sending word by the servant you are not at home—all these are little things. Sometimes you can brace yourself up against a great temptation; and almost before you know it you fall before some little thing. A great many men are overcome by a little persecution.

Persecution.

Do you know, I don't think we have enough persecution now-a-days. Some people say we have persecution that is just as hard to bear as in the Dark Ages. Anyway, I think it would be a good thing if we had a little of the old fashioned kind just now. It would bring out the strongest characters, and make us all healthier. I have heard men get up in prayer-meeting, and say they were going to make a few remarks, and then keep on till you would think they were going to talk all week. If we had a little persecution, people of that kind wouldn't talk so much. Spurgeon used to say some Christians would make good martyrs; they would burn well, they are so dry. If there were a few stakes for burning Christians, I think it would take all the piety out of some men. I admit they haven't got much; but then if they are not willing to suffer a little persecution for Christ, they are not fit to be His disciples. We are told: "All that will live godly in Christ Jesus shall suffer persecution." Make up your mind to this: If the world has nothing to say against you, Jesus Christ will have nothing to say for you.

The most glorious triumphs of the Church have been won in times of persecution. The early church was persecuted for about three hundred years after the crucifixion, and they were years of growth and progress. But then, as Saint Augustine has said, the cross passed from the scene of public executions to the diadem of the Caesars, and the down-grade movement began. When the Church has joined hands with the State, it has invariably retrograded in spirituality and effectiveness; but the opposition of the State has only served to purify it of all dross. It was persecution that gave Scotland to Presbyterianism. It was persecution that gave this country to civil and religious freedom.

How are we to overcome in time of persecution? Hear the words of Christ: "In the world ye shall have tribulation: but be of good cheer: I have overcome the world." Paul could testify that though persecuted, he was never forsaken; that the Lord stood by him, and strengthened him, and delivered him out of all his persecutions and afflictions.

A great many shrink from the Christian life because they will be sneered at. And then, sometimes when persecution won't bring a man down, flattery will. Foolish persons often come up to a man after he has preached and flatter him. Sometimes ladies do that. Perhaps they will say to some worker in the church: "You talk a great deal better than so-and-so"; and he becomes proud, and begins to strut around as if he was the most important person in the town. I tell you, we have a wily devil to contend with. If he can't overcome you with opposition, he will try flattery or ambition; and if that doesn't serve his purpose, perhaps there will come some affliction or disappointment, and he will overcome in way. But remember that anyone that has got Christ to help him can overcome every foe, and overcome them singly or collectively. Let them come. If we have got Christ within us, we will overthrow them all. Remember what Christ is able to do. In all the ages men have stood in greater temptations than you and I will ever have to meet.

Now, there is one more thing on this line: I have either got to overcome the world, or the world is going to overcome me. I have either got to conquer sin in me—or sin about me—and get it under my feet, or it is going to conquer me. A good many people are satisfied with one or two victories, and think that is all. I tell you, my dear friends, we have got to do something more than that. It is a battle all the time. We have this to encourage us: we are assured of victory at the end. We are promised a glorious triumph.

Eight "Overcomes."

Let me give you the eight "overcomes" of Revelation.

The first is: "To him that overcometh will I give to eat of the tree of life." He shall have a right to the tree of life. When Adam fell, he lost that right. God turned him out of Eden lest he should eat of the tree of life and live as he was forever. Perhaps He just took that tree and transplanted it to the Garden above; and through the second Adam we are to have the right to eat of it.

Second: "He that overcometh shall not be hurt of the second death." Death has no terrors for him, it cannot touch him. Why? Because Christ tasted death for every man. Hence he is on resurrection ground. Death may take this body, but that is all. This is only the house I live in. We need have no fear of death if we overcome.

Third: "To him that overcometh will I give to eat of the hidden manna, and will give him a white stone, and in the stone a new name written, which no man knoweth saving he that receiveth it." If I overcome God will feed me with bread that the world knows nothing about, and give me a new name.

Fourth: "He that overcometh, and keepeth My works unto the end, to him will I give power over the nations." Think of it! What a thing to have; power over the nations! A man that is able to rule himself is the man that God can trust with power. Only a man who can govern himself is fit to govern other men. I have an idea that we are down here in training, that God is just polishing us for some higher service. I don't know where the kingdoms are, but it we are to be kings and priests we must have kingdoms to reign over.

Fifth: "He that overcometh, the same shall be clothed in white raiment; and I will not blot out his name out of the book of life, but I will confess his name before My Father, and before His angels." He shall present us to the Father in white garments, without spot or wrinkle. Every fault and stain shall be taken out, and we be made perfect. He that overcomes will not be a stranger in heaven.

Sixth: "Him that overcometh will I make a pillar in the temple of My God; and he shall go no more out; and I will write upon him the name of My God and the name of the city of My God, which is New Jerusalem, which cometh down out of heaven from My God: and I will write upon him My new name." Think of it! No more backsliding, no more wanderings over the dark mountains of sin, but forever with the King, and He says, "I will write upon him the name of My God." He is going to put His name upon us. Isn't it grand? Isn't it worth fighting for? It is said when Mahomet came in sight of Damascus and found that they had all left the city, he said: "If they won't fight for this city what will they fight for?" If men won't fight here for all this reward, what will they fight for?

Seventh: "To him that overcometh will I grant to sit with Me in My throne, even as I also overcame, and am set down with My Father in His throne." My heart has often melted as I have looked at that. The Lord of Glory coming down and saying: "I will grant to you to sit on My throne, even as I sit on My Father's throne, if you will just overcome." Isn't it worth a struggle? How many will fight for a crown that is going to fade away! Yet we are to be placed above the angels, above the archangels, above the seraphim, above the cherubim, away up, upon the throne with Himself, and there we shall be forever with Him. May God put strength into every one of us to fight the battle of life, so that we may sit with Him on His throne. When Frederick of Germany was dying, his own son would not have been allowed to sit with him on the throne, nor to have let anyone else sit there with him. Yet we are told that we are joint heirs with Jesus Christ, and that we are to sit with Him in glory!

And now, the last I like best of all: "He that overcometh shall inherit all things; and I will be his God, and he shall be My son." My dear friends, isn't that a high calling? I used to have my Sabbath-school children sing—"I want to be an angel": but I have not done so for years. We shall be above angels: we shall be sons of God. Just see what a kingdom we shall come into: we shall inherit all things! Do you ask me how much I am worth? I don't know. The Rothschilds cannot compute their wealth. They don't know how many millions they own. That is my condition—I haven't the slightest idea how much I am worth. God has no poor children. If we overcome we shall inherit all things.

Oh, my dear friends, what an inheritance! Let us then get the victory, through Jesus Christ our Lord and Master.

RESULTS OF TRUE REPENTANCE.

I want to call your attention to what true repentance leads to. I am not addressing the unconverted only, because I am one of those who believe that there is a good deal of repentance to be done by the Church before much good will be accomplished in the world. I firmly believe that the low standard of Christian living is keeping a good many in the world and in their sins. When the ungodly see that Christian people do not repent, you cannot expect them to repent and turn away from their sins. I have repented ten thousand times more since I knew Christ than ever before; and I think most Christians have some things to repent of.

So now I want to preach to Christians as well as to the unconverted; to myself as well as to one who has never accepted Christ as his Savior.

There are five things that flow out of true repentance:
1. Conviction.

2. Contrition.

3. Confession of sin.

4. Conversion.

5. Confession of Jesus Christ before the world.

1. Conviction.

When a man is not deeply convicted of sin, it is a pretty sure sign that he has not truly repented. Experience has taught me that men who have very slight conviction of sin, sooner or later lapse back into their old life. For the last few years I have been a good deal more anxious for a deep and true work in professing converts than I have for great numbers. If a man professes to be converted without realizing the heinousness of his sins, he is likely to be one of those stony ground hearers who don't amount to anything. The first breath of opposition, the first wave of persecution or ridicule, will suck them back into the world again.

I believe we are making a woeful mistake in taking so many people into the Church who have never been truly convicted of sin. Sin is just as black in a man's heart to-day as it ever was. I sometimes think it is blacker. For the more light a man has, the greater his responsibility, and therefore the greater need of deep conviction.

William Dawson once told this story to illustrate how humble the soul must be before it can find peace.

He said that at a revival meeting, a little lad who was used to Methodist ways, went home to his mother and said,

"Mother, John So-and-so is under conviction and seeking for peace, but he will not find it to-night, mother."

"Why, William?" said she.

"Because he is only down on one knee, mother, and he will never get peace until he is down on both knees."

Until conviction of sin brings us down on both knees, until we are completely humbled, until we have no hope in ourselves left, we cannot find the Savior.

There are three things that lead to conviction: (1) Conscience; (2) the Word of God; (3) the Holy Spirit. All three are used by God.

Long before we had any Word, God dealt with men through the conscience. That is what made Adam and Eve hide themselves from the presence of the Lord God amongst the trees of the Garden of Eden. That is what convicted Joseph's brethren when they said: "We are verily guilty concerning our brother in that we saw the anguish of his soul when he besought us and we would not hear. Therefore," said they (and remember, over twenty years had passed away since they had sold him into captivity), "therefore is this distress come upon us." That is what we must use with our children before they are old enough to understand about the Word and the Spirit of God. This is what accuses or excuses the heathen.

Conscience is "a divinely implanted faculty in man, telling him that he ought to do right." Someone has said that it was born when Adam and Eve ate of the forbidden fruit, when their eyes were opened and they "knew good and evil." It passes judgment, without being invited, upon our thoughts, words, and actions, approving or condemning according as it judges them to be right or wrong. A man cannot violate his conscience without being self-condemned.

But conscience is not a safe guide, because very often it will not tell you a thing is wrong until you have done it. It needs illuminating by God because it partakes of our fallen nature. Many a person does things that are wrong without being condemned by conscience. Paul said: "I verily thought with myself that I ought to do many things contrary to the name of Jesus of Nazareth." Conscience itself needs to be educated.

Again, conscience is too often like an alarm clock, which awakens and arouses at first, but after a time the man becomes used to it, and it loses its effect. Conscience can be smothered. I think we make a mistake in not preaching more to the conscience.

Hence, in due time, conscience was superseded by the law of God, which in time was fulfilled in Christ.

In this Christian land, where men have Bibles, these are the agency by which God produces conviction. The old Book tells you what is right and wrong before you commit sin, and what you need is to learn and appropriate its teachings, under the guidance of the Holy Spirit. Conscience compared with the Bible is as a rushlight compared with the sun in the heavens.

See how the truth convicted those Jews on the day of Pentecost. Peter, filled with the Holy Ghost, preached that "God hath made this same Jesus, whom ye have crucified, both Lord and Christ." "Now when they heard this, they were pricked in their heart, and said unto Peter and to the rest of the apostles, Men and brethren, what shall we do?"

Then, thirdly, the Holy Ghost convicts. I once heard the late Dr. A. J. Gordon expound that passage—"And when

He (the Comforter) is come, He will reprove the world of sin, of righteousness, and of judgment; of sin because they believe not on Me,"—as follows:—

"Some commentators say there was no real conviction of sin in the world until the Holy Ghost came. I think that foreign missionaries will say that that is not true, that a heathen who never heard of Christ may have a tremendous conviction of sin. For notice that God gave conscience first, and gave the Comforter afterward. Conscience bears witness to the law, the Comforter bears witness to Christ. Conscience brings legal conviction, the Comforter brings evangelical conviction. Conscience brings conviction unto condemnation, and the Comforter brings conviction unto justification. 'He shall convince the world of sin, because they believe not on Me.' That is the sin about which He convinces. It does not say that He convinces men of sin, because they have stolen or lied or committed adultery; but the Holy Ghost is to convince men of sin because they have not believed on Jesus Christ. The coming of Jesus Christ into the world made a sin possible that was not possible before. Light reveals darkness; it takes whiteness to bring conviction concerning blackness. There are negroes in Central Africa who never dreamed that they were black until they saw the face of a white man; and there are a great many people in this world that never knew they were sinful until they saw the face of Jesus Christ in all its purity.

Jesus Christ now stands between us and the law. He has fulfilled the law for us. He has settled all claims of the law, and now whatever claim it had upon us has been transferred to Him, so that it is no longer the sin question, but the Son question, that confronts us. And, therefore, you notice that the first thing Peter does when he begins to preach after the Holy Ghost has been sent down is about

Christ: 'Him being delivered by the determinate counsel of God, ye have taken and by wicked hands have crucified and slain.' It doesn't say a word about any other kind of sin. That is the sin that runs all through Peter's teaching, and as he preached, the Holy Ghost came down and convicted them, and they cried out, 'What shall we do to be saved?'

Well, but we had no part in crucifying Christ; therefore, what is our sin? It is the same sin in another form. They were convicted of crucifying Christ; we are convicted because we have not believed on Christ crucified. They were convicted because they had despised and rejected God's Son. The Holy Ghost convicts us because we have not believed in the Despised and Rejected One. It is really the same sin in both cases—the sin of unbelief in Christ."

Some of the most powerful meetings I have ever been in were those in which there came a sort of hush over the people, and it seemed as if an unseen power gripped their consciences. I remember a man coming to one meeting, and the moment he entered, he felt that God was there. There came an awe upon him, and that very hour he was convicted and converted.

2. Contrition.

The next thing is contrition, deep Godly sorrow and humiliation of heart because of sin. If there is not true contrition, a man will turn right back into the old sin. That is the trouble with many Christians.

A man may get angry, and if there is not much contrition, the next day he will get angry again. A daughter may say mean, cutting things to her mother, and then her conscience troubles her, and she says:

"Mother, I am sorry: forgive me."

But soon there is another outburst of temper, because the contrition is not deep and real. A husband speaks sharp words to his wife, and then to ease his conscience, he goes and buys her a bouquet of flowers. He will not go like a man and say he has done wrong.

What God wants is contrition, and if there is not contrition, there is not full repentance. "The Lord is nigh to the broken of heart, and saveth such as be contrite of spirit." "A broken and a contrite heart, O God, Thou wilt not despise." Many sinners are sorry for their sins, sorry that they cannot continue in sin; but they repent only with hearts that are not broken. I don't think we know how to repent now-a-days. We need some John the Baptist, wandering through the land, crying: "Repent! repent!"

3. Confession of Sin.

If we have true contrition, that will lead us to confess our sins. I believe that nine-tenths of the trouble in our Christian life comes from failing to do this. We try to hide and cover up our sins; there is very little confession of them. Someone has said: "Unconfessed sin in the soul is like a bullet in the body."

If you have no power, it may be there is some sin that needs to be confessed, something in your life that needs straightening out. There is no amount of psalm-singing, no amount of attending religious meetings, no amount of praying or reading your Bible that is going to cover up anything of that kind. It must be confessed, and if I am too proud to confess, I need expect no mercy from God and no answers to my prayers. The Bible says: "He that covereth his sins shall not prosper." He may be a man in the pulpit, a priest behind the altar, a king on the throne; I don't care who he is. Man has been trying it for six thousand years. Adam tried it, and failed. Moses tried it when he buried the Egyptian whom he killed, but he failed. "Be sure your sin will find you out." You cannot bury your sin so deep but it will have a resurrection by and by, if it has not been blotted out by the Son of God. What man has failed to do for six thousand years, you and I had better give up trying to do.

There are three ways of confessing sin. All sin is against God, and must be confessed to Him. There are some sins I need never confess to anyone on earth. If the sin has been between myself and God, I may confess it alone in my closet: I need not whisper it in the ear of any mortal. "Father, I have sinned against heaven, and before Thee." "Against Thee, Thee only, have I sinned, and done this evil in Thy sight."

But if I have done some man a wrong, and he knows that I have wronged him, I must confess that sin not only to God but also to that man. If I have too much pride to confess it to him, I need not come to God. I may pray, and I may weep, but it will do no good. First confess to that man, and then go to God and see how quickly He will hear you, and send peace. "If thou bring thy gift to the altar, and there rememberest that thy brother hath aught against thee; leave there thy gift before the altar, and go thy ways. First be reconciled to thy brother, and then come and offer thy gift." That is the Scripture way.

Then there is another class of sins that must be confessed publicly. Suppose I have been known as a blasphemer, a drunkard, or a reprobate. If I repent of my sins, I owe the public a confession. The confession should be as public as the transgression. Many a person will say some mean thing about another in the presence of others, and then try to patch it up by going to that person alone. The confession should be made so that all who heard the transgression can hear it.

We are good at confessing other people's sins, but if it is true repentance, we shall have as much as we can do to look after our own. When a man or woman gets a good look into God's looking glass, he is not finding fault with other people: he has as much as he can do at home.

"If we confess our sins, He is faithful and just to forgive us our sins, and to cleanse us from all unrighteousness." Thank God for the Gospel! Church member, if there is any sin in your life, make up your mind that you will confess it, and be forgiven. Do not have any cloud between you and God. Be able to read your title clear to the mansion Christ has gone to prepare for you.

4. Conversion.

Confession leads to true conversion, and there is no conversion at all until these three steps have been taken.

Now the word "conversion" means two things. We say a man is "converted" when he is born again. But it also has a different meaning in the Bible. Peter said: "Repent, and be converted." The Revised Version reads: "Repent, and turn." Paul said that he was not disobedient unto the heavenly vision, but began to preach to Jews and Gentiles that they should repent and turn to God. Some old divine has said: "Every man is born with his back to God. Repentance is a change of one's course. It is right about face."

Sin is a turning away from God. As someone has said, it is aversion from God and conversion to the world: and true repentance means conversion to God and aversion from the world. When there is true contrition, the heart is broken for sin; when there is true conversion, the heart is broken from sin. We leave the old life, we are translated out of the kingdom of darkness into the kingdom of light. Wonderful, isn't it?

Unless our repentance includes this conversion, it is not worth much. If a man continues in sin, it is proof of an idle profession. It is like pumping away continually at the ship's pumps, without stopping the leaks. Solomon said:—"If they pray, and confess thy name, and turn from their sin . . ." Prayer and confession would be of no avail while they continued in sin. Let us heed God's call; let us forsake the old wicked way; let us return unto the Lord, and He will have mercy upon us; and to our God, for He will abundantly pardon.

If you have never turned to God, turn now. I have no sympathy with the idea that it takes six months, or six weeks, or six hours to be converted. It doesn't take you very long to turn around, does it? If you know you are wrong, then turn right about.

5. Confession of Christ.

If you are converted, the next step is confess it openly. Listen: "If thou shalt confess with thy mouth the Lord Jesus Christ, and shalt believe in thine heart that God hath raised Him from the dead, thou shalt be saved. For with the heart man believeth unto righteousness, and with the mouth confession is made unto salvation."

Confession of Christ is the culmination of the work of true repentance. We owe it to the world, to our fellow-Christians, to ourselves. He died to redeem us, and shall we be ashamed or afraid to confess Him? Religion as an abstraction, as a doctrine, has little interest for the world, but what people can say from personal experience always has weight.

I remember some meetings being held in a locality where the tide did not rise very quickly, and bitter and reproachful things were being said about the work. But one day, one of the most prominent men in the place rose and said:

"I want it to be known that I am a disciple of Jesus Christ; and if there is any odium to be cast on His cause, I am prepared to take my share of it."

It went through the meeting like an electric current, and a blessing came at once to his own soul and to the souls of others.

Men come to me and say: "Do you mean to affirm, Mr. Moody, that I've got to make a public confession when I accept Christ; do you mean to say I've got to confess Him in my place of business, and in my family? Am I to let the whole world know that I am on His side?"

That is precisely what I mean. A great many are willing to accept Christ, but they are not willing to publish it, to confess it. A great many are looking at the lions and the bears in the way. Now, my friends, the devil's mountains are only made of smoke. He can throw a straw into your path and make a mountain of it. He says to you: "You cannot confess and pray to your family; why, you'll break down! You cannot tell it to your shopmate; he will laugh at you." But when you accept Christ, you will have power to confess Him.

There was a young man in the West—it was the West in those days—who had been more or less interested about his soul's salvation. One afternoon, in his office, he said:

"I will accept Jesus Christ as my Lord and Savior."

He went home and told his wife (who was a nominal professor of religion) that he had made up his mind to serve Christ; and he added:

"After supper to-night I am going to take the company into the drawing-room, and erect the family altar."

"Well," said his wife, "you know some of the gentlemen who are coming to tea are sceptics, and they are older than you are, and don't you think you had better wait until after they have gone, or else go out in the kitchen and have your first prayer with the servants?"

The young man thought for a few moments, and then he said:

"I have asked Jesus Christ into my house for the first time, and I shall take Him into the best room, not into the kitchen."

So he called his friends into the drawing room. There was a little sneering, but he read and prayed. That man afterwards became Chief Justice of the United States Court. Never be ashamed of the Gospel of Christ: it is the power of God unto salvation.

A young man enlisted, and was sent to his regiment. The first night he was in the barracks with about fifteen other young men who passed the time playing cards and gambling. Before retiring, he fell on his knees and prayed, and they began to curse him and jeer at him and throw boots at him.

So it went on the next night and the next, and finally the young man went and told the chaplain what had taken place, and asked what he should do.

"Well," said the chaplain, "you are not at home now, and the other men have just as much right in the barracks as you have. It makes them mad to hear you pray, and the Lord will hear you just as well if you say your prayers in bed and don't provoke them."

For weeks after the chaplain did not see the young man again, but one day he met him, and asked—

"By the way, did you take my advice?"

"I did, for two or three nights."

"How did it work?"

"Well," said the young man, "I felt like a whipped hound, and the third night I got out of bed, knelt down and prayed."

"Well," asked the chaplain, "how did that work?"

The young soldier answered: "We have a prayer-meeting there now every night, and three have been converted, and we are praying for the rest."

Oh, friends, I am so tired of weak Christianity. Let us be out and out for Christ; let us give no uncertain sound. If the world wants to call us fools, let them do it. It is only a little while; the crowning day is coming. Thank God for the privilege we have of confessing Christ.

TRUE WISDOM.

"They that be wise shall shine as the brightness of the firmament; and they that turn many to righteousness as the stars for ever and ever." Dan. 12:3.

That is the testimony of an old man, and one who had the richest and deepest experience of any man living on the face of the earth at the time. He was taken down to Babylon when a young man; some Bible students think he was not more than twenty years of age. If anyone had said, when this young Hebrew was carried away into captivity, that he would outrank all the mighty men of that day—that all the generals who had been victorious in almost every nation at that time were to be eclipsed by this young slave—probably no one would have believed it. Yet for five hundred years no man whose life is recorded in history shone as did this man. He outshone Nebuchadnezzar, Belshazzar, Cyrus, Darius, and all the princes and mighty monarchs of his day.

We are not told when he was converted to a knowledge of the true God, but I think we have good reason to believe that he had been brought under the influence of Jeremiah the prophet. Evidently some earnest, godly man, and no worldly professor, had made a deep impression upon him. Someone had at any rate taught him how he was to serve God.

We hear people nowadays talking about the hardness of the field where they labor; they say their position is a very peculiar one. Think of the field in which Daniel had to work. He was not only a slave, but he was held captive by a nation that detested the Hebrews. The language was unknown to him. There he was among idolaters; yet he commenced at once to shine. He took his stand for God from the very first, and so he went on through his whole life. He gave the dew of his youth to God, and he continued faithful right on till his pilgrimage was ended.

Notice that all those who have made a deep impression on the world, and have shone most brightly have been men who lived in a dark day. Look at Joseph; he was sold as a slave into Egypt by the Ishmaelites; yet he took his God with him into captivity, as Daniel afterwards did. And he remained true to the last; he did not give up his faith because he had been taken away from home and placed among idolaters. He stood firm, and God stood by him.

Look at Moses who turned his back upon the gilded palaces of Egypt, and identified himself with his despised and down-trodden nation. If a man ever had a hard field it was Moses; yet he shone brightly, and never proved unfaithful to his God.

Elijah lived in a far darker day than we do. The whole nation was going over to idolatry. Ahab and his queen, and all the royal court were throwing their influence against the worship of the true God. Yet Elijah stood firm, and shone brightly in that dark and evil day. How his name stands out on the page of history!

Look at John the Baptist. I used to think I would like to live in the days of the prophets; but I have given up that idea. You may be sure that when a prophet appears on the scene, everything is dark, and the professing Church of God has gone over to the service of the god of this world. So it was when John the Baptist made his appearance. See how his name shines out to-day! Eighteen centuries have rolled away, and yet the fame of that wilderness preacher shines brighter than ever. He was looked down upon in his day and generation, but he has outlived all his enemies; his name will be revered and his work remembered as long as the Church is on the earth.

Talk about your field being a hard one! See how Paul shone for God as he went out, the first missionary to the heathen, telling them of the God whom he served, and who had sent His Son to die a cruel death in order to save the world. Men reviled him and his teachings; they laughed him to scorn when he spoke of the crucified One. But he went on preaching the Gospel of the Son of God. He was regarded as a poor tent-maker by the great and mighty ones of his day; but no one can now tell the name of any of his persecutors, or of those who lived at that time, unless their names happen to be associated with his, and they were brought into contact with him.

Now the fact is, all men like to shine. We may as well acknowledge it at once. Go into business circles, and see how men struggle to get into the front rank. Everyone wants to outshine his neighbor and to stand at the head of his profession. Go into the political world, and see how there is a struggle going on as to who shall be the greatest. If you go into a school, you find that there is a rivalry among the boys and girls. They all want to stand at the top of the class. When a boy does reach this position and outranks all the rest, the mother is very proud of it. She will manage to tell all the neighbors how Johnnie has got on, and what a number of prizes he has gained.

Go into the army and you find the same thing—one trying to outstrip the other; everyone is very anxious to shine and rise above his comrades. Go among the young men in their games, and see how anxious the one is to outdo the other. So we have all that desire in us; we like to shine above our fellows.

And yet there are very few who can really shine in the world. Once in a while one man will outstrip all his competitors. Every four years what a struggle goes on throughout our country as to who shall be the President of the United States, the battle raging for six months or a year. Yet only one man can get the prize. There are a good many struggling to get the place, but many are disappointed, because only one can attain the coveted prize. But in the kingdom of God the very least and the very weakest may shine if they will. Not only can one obtain the prize, but all may have it if they will.

It does not say in this passage that the statesmen are going to shine as the brightness of the firmament. The statesmen of Babylon are gone; their very names are forgotten.

It does not say that the nobility are going to shine. Earth's nobility are soon forgotten. John Bunyan, the Bedford tinker, has outlived the whole crowd of those who were the nobility in his day. They lived for self, and their memory is blotted out. He lived for God and for souls, and his name is as fragrant as ever it was.

We are not told that the merchants are going to shine. Who can tell the name of any of the millionaires of Daniel's day? They were all buried in oblivion a few years after their death. Who were the mighty conquerors of that day? But few can tell. It is true that we hear of Nebuchadnezzar, but probably we should not have known very much about him but of his relations to the prophet Daniel.

How different with this faithful prophet of the Lord! Twenty five centuries have passed away, and his name shines on, and on, and on, brighter and brighter. And it is going to shine while the Church of God exists. "They that be wise shall shine as the brightness of the firmament; and they that turn many to righteousness as the stars forever and ever."

How quickly the glory of this world fades away! Eighty years ago the great Napoleon almost made the earth to tremble. How he blazed and shone as an earthly warrior for a little while! A few years passed and a little island held that once proud and mighty conqueror; he died a poor broken-hearted prisoner. Where is he to-day? Almost forgotten. Who in all the world will say that Napoleon lives in their heart's affections?

But look at this despised and hated Hebrew prophet. They wanted to put him into the lions' den because he was too sanctimonious and too religious Yet see how green his memory is to-day! How his name is loved and honored for his faithfulness to his God.

Many years ago I was in Paris, at the time of the Great Exhibition. Napoleon the Third was then in his glory. Cheer after cheer would rise as he drove along the streets of the city. A few short years, and he fell from his lofty estate. He died an exile from his country and his throne, and where is his name today? Very few think about him at all, and if his name is mentioned it is not with love and esteem. How empty and short lived are the glory and the pride of this world! If we are wise, we will live for God and eternity; we will get outside of ourselves, and will care nothing for the honor and glory of this world. In Proverbs we read: "He that winneth souls is wise." If any man, woman, or child by a Godly life and example can win one soul to God, their life will not have been a failure. They will have outshone all the mighty men of their day, because they will have set a stream in motion that will flow on and on forever and ever.

God has left us down here to shine. We are not here to buy and sell and get gain, to accumulate wealth, to acquire worldly position. This earth, if we are Christians, is not our home; it is up yonder. God has sent us into the world to shine for Him—to light up this dark world. Christ came to be the Light of the world, but men put out that light. They took it to Calvary, and blew it out. Before Christ went up on high, He said to His disciples: "Ye are the light of the world. Ye are my witnesses. Go forth and carry the Gospel to the perishing nations of the earth."

So God has called us to shine, just as much as Daniel was sent into Babylon to shine. Let no man or woman say that they cannot shine because they have not so much influence as some others may have. What God wants you to do is to use the influence you have. Daniel probably did not have much influence down in Babylon at first, but God soon gave him more, because he was faithful and used what he had.

Remember a small light will do a good deal when it is in a very dark place. Put one little tallow candle in the middle of a large hall, and it will give a good deal of light.

Away out in the prairie regions, when meetings are held at night in the log schoolhouses, the announcement of the meeting is given out in this way:

"A meeting will be held by early candlelight."

The first man who comes brings a tallowdip with him. It is perhaps all he has; but he brings it, and sets it on the desk. It does not light the building much; but it is better than nothing at all. The next man brings his candle; and the next family bring theirs. By the time the house is full, there is plenty of light. So if we all shine a little, there will be a good deal of light. That is what God wants us to do. If we cannot all be lighthouses, any one of us can at any rate be a tallow candle.

A little light will sometimes do a great deal. The city of Chicago was set on fire by a cow kicking over a lamp, and a hundred thousand people were burnt out of house and home. Do not let Satan get the advantage of you, and make you think that because you cannot do any great thing you cannot do anything at all.

Then we must remember that we are to let our light shine. It does not say, "Make your light shine." You do not have to make light to shine; all you have to do is to let it shine.

I remember hearing of a man at sea who was very seasick. If there is a time when a man feels that he cannot do any work for the Lord it is then—in my opinion. While this man was sick, he heard that someone had fallen overboard. He was wondering if he could do anything to help to save the man. He laid hold of a light, and held it up to the port-hole. The drowning man was saved. When this man got over his attack of sickness, he went on deck one day and was talking with the man who was rescued. The saved man gave this testimony. He said he had gone down the second time, and was just going down again for the last time, when he put out his hand. Just then, he said, someone held a light at the port-hole, and the light fell on it. A sailor caught him by the hand and pulled him into the lifeboat.

It seemed a small thing to do to hold up the light; yet it saved the man's life. If you cannot do some great thing you can hold the light for some poor, perishing drunkard, who may be won to Christ and delivered from destruction. Let us take the torch of salvation and go into the dark homes, and hold up Christ to the people as the Savior of the world. If the perishing masses are to be reached, we must lay our lives right alongside theirs, and pray with them and labor for them. I would not give much for a man's Christianity if he is saved himself and is not willing to try and save others. It seems to me the basest ingratitude if we do not reach out the hand to others who are down in the same pit from which we were delivered. Who is able to reach and help drinking men like those who have themselves been slaves to the intoxicating cup? Will you not go out this very day and seek to rescue these men? If we were all to do what we can, we should soon empty the drinking saloons.

I remember reading of a blind man who was found sitting at the corner of a street in a great city with a lantern beside him. Someone went up to him and asked what he had the lantern there for, seeing that he was blind, and the light was the same to him as the darkness. The blind man replied:

"I have it so that no one may stumble over me."

Dear friends, let us think of that. Where one man reads the Bible, a hundred read you and me. That is what Paul meant when he said we were to be living epistles of Christ, known and read of all men. I would not give much for all that can be done by sermons, if we do not preach Christ by our lives. If we do not commend the Gospel to people by our holy walk and conversation, we shall not win them to Christ. Some little act of kindness will perhaps do more to influence them than any number of long sermons.

A vessel was caught in a storm on Lake Erie, and they were trying to make for the harbor of Cleveland. At the entrance of that port they had what are called the upper lights and the lower lights. Away back on the bluffs were the upper lights burning brightly enough; but when they came near the harbor they could not see the lights showing the entrance to it. The pilot said he thought they had better get back on the lake again. The Captain said he was sure they would go down if they went back, and he urged the pilot to do what he could to gain the harbor. The pilot said there was very little hope of making the harbor, as he had nothing to guide him as to how he should steer the ship. They tried all they could to get her in. She rode on the top of the waves, and then into the trough of the sea, and at last they found themselves stranded on the beach, where the vessel was dashed to pieces. Someone had neglected the lower lights, and they had gone out.

Let us take warning. God keeps the upper lights burning as brightly as ever, but He has left us down here to keep the lower lights burning. We are to represent Him here, as Christ represents us up yonder. I sometimes think if we had as poor a representative in the courts above as God has down here on earth, we would have a pretty poor chance of heaven. Let us have our loins girt and our lights brightly burning, so that others may see the way and not walk in darkness.

Speaking of a lighthouse reminds me of what I heard about a man in the State of Minnesota, who, some years ago, was caught in a fearful storm. That State is cursed with storms which come sweeping down so suddenly in the winter time that escape is difficult. The snow will fall and the wind will beat it into the face of the traveler so that he cannot see two feet ahead. Many a man has been lost on the prairies when he has got caught in one of those storms.

This man was caught and was almost on the point of giving up, when he saw a little light in a log house. He managed to get there, and found a shelter from the fury of the tempest. He is now a wealthy man. As soon as he was able, he bought the farm, and built a beautiful house on the spot where the log building stood. On the top of a tower he put a revolving light, and every night when there comes a storm he lights it up in the hope that it may be the means of saving someone else.

That is true gratitude, and that is what God wants us to do. If He has rescued us and brought us up out of the horrible pit, let us be always looking to see if there is not someone else whom we can help to save.

I remember hearing of two men who had charge of a revolving light in a lighthouse on a rock-bound and stormy coast. Somehow the machinery went wrong, and the light did not revolve. They were so afraid that those at sea should mistake it for some other light, that they worked all the night through to keep the light moving round.

Let us keep our lights in the proper place, so that the world may see that the religion of Christ is not a sham but a reality. It is said that in the Grecian sports they had one game where the men ran with lights. They lit a torch at the altar, and ran a certain distance; sometimes they were on horseback. If a man came in with his light still burning, he received a prize; if his light had gone out, he lost the prize.

How many there are who, in their old age, have lost their light and their joy! They were once burning and shining lights in the family, in the Sunday-school, and in the Church. But something has come in between them and God—the world or self—and their light has gone out. Reader, if you are one who has had this experience, may God help you to come back to the altar of the Savior's love and light up your torch anew, so that you can go out into the lanes and alleys, and let the light of the Gospel shine in these dark homes.

As I have already said, if we only lead one soul to Jesus Christ we may set a stream in motion that will flow on when we are dead and gone. Away up the mountain side there is a little spring; it seems so small that an ox might drink it up at a draught. By and by it becomes a rivulet; other rivulets run into it. Before long it is a large brook, and then it becomes a broad river sweeping onward to the sea. On its banks are cities, towns and villages, where many thousands live. Vegetation flourishes on every side, and commerce is carried down its stately bosom to distant lands.

So if you turn one to Christ, that one may turn a hundred; they may turn a thousand, and so the stream, small at first, goes on broadening and deepening as it rolls toward eternity.

In the book of Revelation we read: "I heard a voice from heaven saying unto me, Write, Blessed are the dead which die in the Lord from henceforth: yea, saith the Spirit, that they may rest from their labors; and their works do follow them."

There are many mentioned in the Scriptures of whom we read that they lived so many years and then they died. The cradle and the grave are brought close together; they lived and they died, and that is all we know about them. So in these days you could write on the tombstone of a great many professing Christians that they were born on such a day and they died on such a day; there is nothing whatever between.

But there is one thing you cannot bury with a good man; his influence still lives. They have not buried Daniel yet: his influence is as great today as it ever was. Do you tell me that Joseph is dead? His influence still lives and will continue to live on and on. You may bury the frail tenement of clay that a good man lives in, but you cannot get rid of his influence and example. Paul was never more powerful than he is to-day.

Do you tell me that John Howard, who went into so many of the dark prisons in Europe, is dead? Is Henry Martyn, or Wilberforce, or John Bunyan dead? Go into the Southern States, and there you will find millions of men and women who once were slaves. Mention to any of them the name of Wilberforce, and see how quickly the eye will light up. He lived for something else besides himself, and his memory will never die out of the hearts of those for whom he lived and labored.

Is Wesley or Whitefield dead? The names of those great evangelists were never more honored than they are now. Is John Knox dead? You can go to any part of Scotland today, and feel the power of his influence.

I will tell you who are dead. The enemies of these servants of God—those who persecuted them and told lies about them. But the men themselves have outlived all the lies that were uttered concerning them. Not only that; they will shine in another world. How true are the words of the old

Book: "They that be wise shall shine as the brightness of the firmament; and they that turn many to righteousness as the stars forever and ever."

Let us go on turning as many as we can to righteousness. Let us be dead to the world, to its lies, its pleasures, and its ambitions. Let us live for God, continually going forth to win souls for Him.

Let me quote a few words by Dr. Chalmers: "Thousands of men breathe, move and live, pass off the stage of life, and are heard no more—Why? They do not partake of good in the world, and none were blessed by them; none could point to them as the means of their redemption; not a line they wrote, not a word they spoke could be recalled; and so they perished; their light went out in darkness, and they were not remembered more than insects of yesterday. Will you thus live and die, O man immortal? Live for something. Do good, and leave behind you a monument of virtue that the storms of time can never destroy. Write your name in kindness, love and mercy, on the hearts of the thousands you come in contact with year by year; you will never be forgotten. No, your name, your deeds will be as legible on the hearts you leave behind as the stars on the brow of evening. Good deeds will shine as the stars of heaven."

"COME THOU AND ALL THY HOUSE INTO THE ARK."

I want to call your attention to a text that you will find in the seventh chapter of Genesis, first verse. When God speaks, you and I can afford to listen. It is not man speaking now, but it is God. "The Lord said unto Noah, Come thou and all thy house into the ark."

Perhaps some sceptic is reading this, and perhaps some church member will join with him and say,

"I hope Mr. Moody is not going to preach about the ark. I thought that was given up by all intelligent people."

But I want to say that I haven't given it up. When I do, I am going to give up the whole Bible. There is hardly any portion of the Old Testament Scripture but that the Son of God set His seal to it when He was down here in the world.

Men say, "I don't believe in the story of the flood."

Christ connected His own return to this world with that flood: "And as it was in the days of Noah, so shall it be also in the days of the Son of man. They did eat, they drank, they married wives, they were given in marriage, until the day that Noah entered into the ark, and the flood came, and destroyed them all."

I believe the story of the flood just as much as I do the third chapter of John. I pity any man that is picking the old Book to pieces. The moment that we give up any one of these things, we touch the deity of the Son of God. I have noticed that when a man does begin to pick the Bible to pieces, it doesn't take him long to tear it all to pieces. What is the use of being five years about what you can do in five minutes?

A Solemn Message.

One hundred and twenty years before God spake the words of my text, Noah had received the most awful communication that ever came from heaven to earth. No man up to that time, and I think no man since, has ever received such a communication. God said that on account of the wickedness of the world He was going to destroy the world by water. We can have no idea of the extent and character of that antediluvian wickedness. The Bible piles one expression on another, in its effort to emphasize it. "God saw that the wickedness of man was great in the earth, and that every imagination of the thoughts of his heart was only evil continually. And it repented the Lord that He had made man on the earth, and it grieved him at His heart. . . . The earth also was corrupt before God, and the earth was filled with violence. And God looked upon the earth, and, behold, it was corrupt; for all flesh had corrupted his way upon the earth." Men lived five hundred years and more then, and they had time to mature in their sins.

How the Message was Received.

For one hundred and twenty years God strove with those antediluvians. He never smites without warning, and they had their warning. Every time Noah drove a nail into the ark it was a warning to them. Every sound of the hammer echoed, "I believe in God." If they had repented and cried as they did at Nineveh, I believe God would have heard their cry and spared them. But there was no cry for mercy. I have no doubt but that they ridiculed the idea that God was going to destroy the world. I have no doubt but that there were atheists who said there was not any God anyhow. I got hold of one of them some time ago. I said,

"How do you account for the formation of the world?"

"Oh! force and matter work together, and by chance the world was created."

I said, "It is a singular thing that your tongue isn't on the top of your head if force and matter just threw it together in that manner."

If I should take out my watch and say that force and matter worked together, and out came the watch, you would say I was a lunatic of the first order. Wouldn't you? And yet they say that this old world was made by chance! "It threw itself together!"

I met a man in Scotland, and he took the ground that there was no God. I asked him,

"How do you account for creation, for all these rocks?" (They have a great many rocks in Scotland.)

"Why!" he said, "any school boy could account for that."

"Well, how was the first rock made?"

"Out of sand."

"How was the first sand made?"

"Out of rock."

You see he had it all arranged so nicely. Sand and rock, rock and sand. I have no doubt but that Noah had these men to contend with.

Then there was a class called agnostics, and there are a good many of their grandchildren, alive to-day. Then there was another class who said they believed there was a God; they couldn't make themselves believe that the world happened by chance; but God was too merciful to punish sin. He was so full of compassion and love that He couldn't punish sin. The drunkard, the harlot, the gambler, the murderer, the thief and the libertine would all share alike with the saints at the end. Supposing the governor of your state was so tender-hearted that he could not bear to have a man suffer, could not bear to see a man put in jail, and he should go and set all the prisoners free. How long would he be governor? You would have him out of office before the sun set. These very men that talk about God's mercy, would be the first to raise a cry against a governor who would not have a man put in prison when he had done wrong.

Then another class took the ground that God could not destroy the world anyway. They might have a great flood which would rise up to the meadowlands and lowlands, but all it would be necessary to do would be to go up on the hills and mountains. That would be a hundred times better than Noah's ark. Or if it should come to that, they could build rafts, which would be a good deal better than that ark. They had never seen such an ugly looking thing. It was about five hundred feet long, and about eighty feet wide, and fifty feet high. It had three stories, and only one small window.

And then, I suppose there was a large class who took the ground that Noah must be wrong because he was in such a minority. That is a great argument now, you know. Noah was greatly in the minority. But he went on working.

If they had saloons then, and I don't doubt but that they had, for we read that there was "violence in the land," and wherever you have alcohol you have violence. We read also that Noah planted a vineyard and fell into the sin of intemperance. He was a righteous man, and if he did that, what must the others have done? Well, if they had saloons, no doubt they sang ribald songs about Noah and his ark, and if they had theaters they likely acted it out, and mothers took their children to see it.

And if they had the press in those days, every now and then there would appear a skit about "Noah and his folly." Reporters would come and interview him, and if they had an Associated Press, every few days a dispatch would be sent out telling how the work on the ark was progressing.

And perhaps they had excursions, and offered as an inducement that people could go through the ark. And if Noah happened to be around they would nudge each other and say:

"That's Noah. Don't you think there is a strange look in his eye?"

As a Scotchman would say, they thought him a little daft. Thank God a man can afford to be mad. A mad man thinks everyone else mad but himself A drunkard does not call himself mad when he is drinking up all his means. Those men who stand and deal out death and damnation to men are not called mad; but a man is called mad when he gets into the ark, and is saved for time and eternity. And I expect if the word crank was in use, they called Noah "an old crank."

And so all manner of sport was made of Noah and his ark. And the business men went on buying and selling, while Noah went on preaching and toiling. They perhaps had some astronomers, and they were gazing up at the stars, and saying, "Don't you be concerned. There is no sign of a coming storm in the heavens. We are very wise men, and if there was a storm coming, we should read it in the heavens." And they had geologists digging away, and they said, "There is no sign in the earth." Even the carpenters who helped build the ark might have made fun of him, but they were like lots of people at the present day, who will help build a church, and perhaps give money for its support, but will never enter it themselves.

Well, things went on as usual. Little lambs skipped on the hillsides each spring. Men sought after wealth, and if they had leases, I expect they ran for longer periods than ours do. We think ninety-nine years a long time, but I don't doubt but that theirs ran for nine hundred and ninety nine years. And when they came to sign a lease they would say with a twinkle in their eyes:

"Why, this old Noah says the world is coming to an end in one hundred and twenty years, and it's twenty years since he started the story. But I guess I will sign the lease and risk it."

Someone has said that Noah must have been deaf, or he could not have stood the jeers and sneers of his countrymen. But if he was deaf to the voice of men, he heard the voice of God when He told him to build the ark.

I can imagine one hundred years have rolled away, and the work on the ark ceases. Men say, "What has he stopped work for?" He has gone on a preaching tour, to tell the people of the coming storm—that God is going to sweep every man from the face of the earth unless he is in the ark. But he cannot get a man to believe him except his own family. Some of the old men have passed away, and they died saying: "Noah is wrong." Poor Noah! He must have had a hard time of it. I don't think I should have had the grace to work for one hundred and twenty years without a convert. But he just toiled on, believing the word of God.

And now the hundred and twenty years are up. In the spring of the year Noah did not plant anything, for he knew the flood was coming, and the people say: "Every year before he has planted, but this year he thinks the world is going to be destroyed, and he hasn't planted anything."

Moving in.

But I can imagine one beautiful morning, not a cloud to be seen, Noah has got his communication. He has heard the voice that he heard one hundred and twenty years before— the same old voice. Perhaps there had been silence for one hundred and twenty years. But the voice rang through his soul once again, "Noah, come thou and all thy house into the ark."

The word "come" occurs about nineteen hundred times in the Bible, it is said, and this is the first time. It meant salvation. You can see Noah and all his family moving into the ark. They are bringing the household furniture.

Some of his neighbors say, "Noah, what is your hurry? you will have plenty of time to get into that old ark. What is your hurry? There are no windows and you cannot look out to see when the storm is coming." But he heard the voice and obeyed.

Some of his relatives might have said, "What are you going to do with the old homestead?"

Noah says, "I don't want it. The storm is coming." He tells them the day of grace is closing, that worldly wealth is of no value, and that the ark is the only place of safety. We must bear in mind that these railroads that we think so much of, will soon go down; they only run for time, not for eternity. The heavens will be on fire, and then what will property, honor, and position in society be worth?

The first thing that alarms them is, they rise one morning, and lo! the heavens are filled with the fowls of the air. They are flying into the ark, two by two. They come from the desert; they come from the mountain; they come from all parts of the world. They are going into the ark. It must have been a strange sight. I can hear the people cry, "Great God! what is the meaning of this?" And they look down on the earth; and, with great alarm and surprise, they see little insects creeping up two by two, coming from all parts of the world. Then behold! there come cattle and beasts, two by two. The neighbors cry out, "What does this mean?" They run to their statesmen and wise men, who have told them there was no sign of a coming storm, and ask them why it is that those birds, animals, and creeping things go toward the ark, as if guided by some unseen hand.

"Well," the statesmen and wise men say, "We cannot explain it; but give yourselves no trouble; God is not going to destroy the world. Business was never better than it is now. Do you think if God was going to destroy the world, He would let us go on so prosperously as He has? There is no sign of a coming storm. What has made these creeping insects and these wild beasts of the forest go into the ark, we do not know. We cannot understand it; it is very strange. But there is no sign of anything going to happen. The stars are bright, and the sun shines as bright as ever it did. Everything moves on as it has been moving for all time past. You can hear the children playing in the street. You can hear the voice of the bride and bridegroom in the land, and all is merry as ever."

I imagine the alarm passed away, and they fell into their regular courses. Noah comes out and says: "The door is going to be shut. Come in. God is going to destroy the world. See the animals, how they have come up. The communication has come to them direct from heaven." But the people only mocked on.

Do you know, when the hundred and twenty years were up, God gave the world seven days' grace? Did you ever notice that? If there had been a cry during those seven days, I believe it would have been heard. But there was none.

At length the last day had come, the last hour, the last minute, ay! the last second. God Almighty came down and shut the door of that ark. No angel, no man, but God Himself shut that door, and when once the master of the house has risen and shut to the door, the doom of the world is sealed; and the doom of that old world was forever sealed. The sun had gone down upon the glory of that old world for the last time. You can hear away off in the distance the mutterings of the storm. You can hear the thunder rolling. The lightning begins to flash, and the old world reels. The storm bursts upon them, and that old ark of Noah's would have been worth more than the whole world to them.

I want to say to any scoffer who reads this, that you can laugh at the Bible, you can scoff at your mother's God, you can laugh at ministers and Christians, but the hour is coming when one promise in that old Book will be worth more to you than ten thousand worlds like this.

The windows of heaven are opened and the fountains of the great deep are broken up. The waters come bubbling up, and the sea bursts its bounds and leaps over its walls. The rivers begin to swell. The people living in the lowlands flee to the mountains and highlands. They flee up the hillsides. And there is a wail going up:

"Noah! Noah! Noah! Let us in."

They leave their homes and come to the ark now. They pound on the ark. Hear them cry:

"Noah! Let us in. Noah! Have mercy on us."

"I am your nephew."

"I am your niece."

"I am your uncle."

Ah, there is a voice inside, saying: "I would like to let you in; but God has shut the door, and I cannot open it!"

God shut that door! When the door is shut, there is no hope. Their cry for mercy was too late; their day of grace was closed. Their last hour had come. God had plead with them; God had invited them to come in; but they had mocked at the invitation. They scoffed and ridiculed the idea of a deluge. Now it is too late.

God did not permit anyone to survive to tell us how they perished. When Job lost his family, there came a messenger to him: but there came no messenger from the antediluvians; not even Noah himself could see the world perish. If he could, he would have seen men and women and children dashing against that ark; the waves rising higher and higher, while those outside were perishing, dying in unbelief. Some think to escape by climbing the trees, and think the storm will soon go down; but it rains on, day and night, for forty days and forty nights, and they are swept away as the waves dash against them. The statesmen and astronomers and great men call for mercy; but it is too late. They had disobeyed the God of mercy. He had called, and they refused. He had plead with them, but they had laughed and mocked. But now the time is come for judgment instead of mercy.

Judgment.

The time is coming again when God will deal in judgment with the world. It is but a little while; we know not when, but it is sure to come. God's word has gone forth that this world shall be rolled together like a scroll, and shall be on fire. What then will become of your soul? It is a loving call, "Now come, thou and all thy house, into the ark." Twenty four hours before the rain began to fall, Noah's ark, if it had been sold at auction, would not have brought as much as it would be worth for kindling wood. But twenty four hours after the rain began to fall, Noah's ark was worth more than all the world. There was not then a man living but would have given all he was worth for a seat in the ark. You may turn away and laugh.

"I believe in Christ!" you say; "I would rather be without Him than have Him."

But bear in mind, the time is coming when Christ will be worth more to you than ten thousand worlds like this. Bear in mind that He is offered to you now. This is a day of grace; it is a day of mercy. You will find, if you read your Bible carefully, that God always precedes judgment with grace. Grace is a forerunner of judgment. He called these men in the days of Noah in love. They would have been saved if they had repented in those one hundred and twenty years. When Christ came to plead with the people in Jerusalem, it was their day of grace; but they mocked and laughed at Him. He said: "O Jerusalem, Jerusalem, thou that killest the prophets, and stonest them which are sent unto thee, how often would I have gathered thy children together, even as a hen gathereth her chickens under her wings, and ye would not!" Forty years afterward, thousands of the people begged that their lives might be spared; and eleven hundred thousand perished in that city.

In 1857 a revival swept over this country in the east and on to the western cities, clear over to the Pacific coast. It was God calling the nation to Himself. Half a million people united with the Church at that time. Then the war broke out. We were baptized with the Holy Ghost in 1857, and in 1861 we were baptized in blood. It was a call of mercy, preceding judgment.

Are Your Children Safe?

The text which I have selected has a special application to Christian people and to parents. This command of the Scripture was given to Noah not only for his own safety, but that of his household, and the question which I put to each father and mother is this: "Are your children in the ark of God?" You may scoff at it, but it is a very important question. Are all your children in? Are all your grandchildren in? Don't rest day or night until you get your children in. I believe my children have fifty temptations where I had one. I am one of those who believe that in the great cities there is a snare set upon the corner of every street for our sons and daughters; and I don't believe it is our business to spend our time in accumulating bonds and stocks. Have I done all I can to get my children in? That is it.

Now, let me ask another question: What would have been Noah's feelings if, when God called him into the ark, his children would not have gone with him? If he had lived such a false life that his children had no faith in his word, what would have been his feelings? He would have said: "There is my poor boy on the mountain. Would to God I had died in his place! I would rather have perished than had him perish." David cried over his son: "Oh, my son Absalom, my son, my son Absalom, would God I had died for thee!" Noah loved his children, and they had confidence in him.

Someone sent me a paper a number of years ago, containing an article that was marked. Its title was: "Are all the children in?" An old wife lay dying. She was nearly one hundred years of age, and the husband who had taken the journey with her, sat by her side. She was just breathing faintly, but suddenly she revived, opened her eyes, and said:

"Why! it is dark."

"Yes, Janet, it is dark."

"Is it night?"

"Oh, yes! it is midnight."

"Are all the children in?"

There was that old mother living life over again. Her youngest child had been in the grave twenty years, but she was traveling back into the old days, and she fell asleep in Christ asking, "Are all the children in?"

Dear friend, are they all in? Put the question to yourself now. Is John in? Is James in? Or is he immersed in business and pleasure? Is he living a double and dishonest life? Say! where is your boy, mother? Where is your son, your daughter? Is it well with your children? Can you say it is?

After being superintendent of a Sunday school in Chicago for a number of years, a school of over a thousand members, children that came from godless homes, having mothers and fathers working against me, taking the children off on excursions on Sunday, and doing all they could to break up the work I was trying to do, I used to think that if I should ever stand before an audience I would speak to no one but parents; that would be my chief business. It is an old saying—"Get the lamb, and you will get the sheep." I gave that up years ago. Give me the sheep, and then I will have someone to nurse the lamb; but get a lamb and convert him, and if he has a godless father and mother, you will have little chance with that child. What we want is godly homes. The home was established long before the Church.

I have no sympathy with the idea that our children have to grow up before they are converted. Once I saw a lady with three daughters at her side, and I stepped up to her and asked her if she was a Christian.

"Yes, sir."

Then I asked the oldest daughter if she was a Christian. The chin began to quiver, and the tears came into her eyes, and she said,

"I wish I was."

The mother looked very angrily at me and said, "I don't want you to speak to my children on that subject. They don't understand." And in great rage she took them all away from me. One daughter was fourteen years old, one twelve, and the other ten, but they were not old enough to be talked to about religion. Let them drift into the world and plunge into worldly amusements, and then see how hard it is to reach them. Many a mother is mourning to-day because her boy has gone beyond her reach, and will not allow her to pray with him. She may pray for him, but he will not let her pray or talk with him. In those early days when his mind was tender and young, she might have led him to Christ. Bring them in. "Suffer the little children to come unto Me." Is there a prayerless father reading this? May God let the arrow go down into your soul! Make up your mind that, God helping you, you will get the children in. God's order is to the father first, but if he isn't true to his duty, then the mother should be true, and save the children from the wreck. Now is the time to do it while you have them under your roof. Exert your parental influence over them.

I never speak to parents but I think of two fathers, one of whom lived on the banks of the Mississippi, the other in New York. The first one devoted all his time to amassing wealth. He had a son to whom he was much attached, and one day the boy was brought home badly injured. The father was informed that the boy could live but a short time, and he broke the news to his son as gently as possible.

"You say I cannot live, father? O! then pray for my soul," said the boy.

In all those years that father had never said a prayer for that boy, and he told him he couldn't. Shortly after, the boy died. That father has said since that he would give all that he possessed if he could call that boy back only to offer one short prayer for him.

The other father had a boy who had been sick some time, and he came home one day and found his wife weeping. She said:

"I cannot help but believe that this is going to prove fatal."

The man started, and said: "If you think so, I wish you would tell him."

But the mother could not tell her boy. The father went to the sick room, and he saw that death was feeling for the cords of life, and he said:

"My son, do you know you are not going to live?"

The little fellow looked up and said: "No; is this death that I feel stealing over me? Will I die to-day?"

"Yes, my son, you cannot live the day out."

And the little fellow smiled and said: "Well, father, I shall be with Jesus tonight, shan't I?"

"Yes, you will spend the night with the Lord," and the father broke down and wept.

The little fellow saw the tears, and said: "Don't weep for me. I will go to Jesus and tell Him that ever since I can remember you have prayed for me."

I have three children, and if God should take them from me, I would rather have them take such a message home to Him than to have the wealth of the whole world. Oh! would to God I could say something to stir you, fathers and mothers, to get your children into the ark.

HUMILITY.

"Learn of me, for I am meek and lowly in heart."—
Matthew 11:29.

There is no harder lesson to learn than the lesson of
humility. It is not taught in the schools of men, only in the
school of Christ. It is the rarest of all the gifts. Very rarely
do we find a man or woman who is following closely the
footsteps of the Master in meekness and in humility. I
believe that it is the hardest lesson which Jesus Christ had
to teach His disciples while He was here upon earth. It
almost looked at first as though He had failed to teach it to
the twelve men who had been with Him almost constantly
for three years.

I believe that if we are humble enough we shall be sure to
get a great blessing. After all, I think that more depends
upon us than upon the Lord, because He is always ready to
give a blessing and give it freely, but we are not always in a
position to receive it. He always blesses the humble, and, if
we can get down in the dust before Him, no one will go
away disappointed. It was Mary at the feet of Jesus, who
had chosen the "better part."

Did you ever notice the reason Christ gave for learning of
Him? He might have said: "Learn of me, because I am the
most advanced thinker of the age. I have performed
miracles that no man else has performed. I have shown my
supernatural power in a thousand ways." But no: the reason
He gave was that He was "meek, and lowly in heart."

We read of the three men in Scripture whose faces shone,
and all three were noted for their meekness and humility.

We are told that the face of Christ shone at His transfiguration; Moses, after he had been in the mount for forty days, came down from his communion with God with a shining face; and when Stephen stood before the Sanhedrim on the day of his death, his face was lighted up with glory. If our faces are to shine we must get into the valley of humility; we must go down in the dust before God.

Bunyan says that it is hard to get down into the valley of humiliation, the descent into it is steep and rugged; but that it is very fruitful and fertile and beautiful when once we get there. I think that no one will dispute that; almost every man, even the ungodly, admires meekness.

Someone asked Augustine, what was the first of the religious graces, and he said, "Humility." They asked him what was the second, and he replied, "Humility." They asked him the third, and he said, "Humility." I think that if we are humble, we have all the graces.

Some years ago I saw what is called a sensitive plant. I happened to breathe on it, and suddenly it drooped its head; I touched it, and it withered away. Humility is as sensitive as that; it cannot safely be brought out on exhibition. A man who is flattering himself that he is humble and is walking close to the Master, is self-deceived. It consists not in thinking meanly of ourselves, but in not thinking of ourselves at all. Moses wist not that his face shone. If humility speaks of itself, it is gone.

Someone has said that the grass is an illustration of this lowly grace. It was created for the lowliest service. Cut it, and it springs up again. The cattle feed upon it, and yet how beautiful it is.

The showers fall upon the mountain peaks, and very often leave them barren because they rush down into the meadows and valleys and make the lowly places fertile. If a man is proud and lifted up, rivers of grace may flow over him and yet leave him barren and unfruitful, while they bring blessing to the man who has been brought low by the grace of God.

A man can counterfeit love, he can counterfeit faith, he can counterfeit hope and all the other graces, but it is very difficult to counterfeit humility. You soon detect mock humility. They have a saying in the East among the Arabs, that as the tares and the wheat grow they show which God has blessed. The ears that God has blessed bow their heads and acknowledge every grain, and the more fruitful they are the lower their heads are bowed. The tares which God has sent as a curse, lift up their heads erect, high above the wheat, but they are only fruitful of evil. I have a pear tree on my farm which is very beautiful; it appears to be one of the most beautiful trees on my place. Every branch seems to be reaching up to the light and stands almost like a wax candle, but I never get any fruit from it. I have another tree, which was so full of fruit last year that the branches almost touched the ground. If we only get down low enough, my friends, God will use every one of us to His glory.

"As the lark that soars the highest builds her nest the lowest; as the nightingale that sings so sweetly, sings in the shade when all things rest; as the branches that are most laden with fruit, bend lowest; as the ship most laden, sinks deepest in the water;—so the holiest Christians are the humblest."

The London Times some years ago told the story of a petition that was being circulated for signatures. It was a time of great excitement, and this petition was intended to have great influence in the House of Lords; but there was one word left out. Instead of reading, "We humbly beseech thee," it read, "We beseech thee." So it was ruled out. My friends, if we want to make an appeal to the God of Heaven, we must humble ourselves; and if we do humble ourselves before the Lord, we shall not be disappointed.

As I have been studying some Bible characters that illustrate humility, I have been ashamed of myself. If you have any regard for me, pray that I may have humility. When I put my life beside the life of some of these men, I say, Shame on the Christianity of the present day. If you want to get a good idea of yourself, look at some of the Bible characters that have been clothed with meekness and humility, and see what a contrast is your position before God and man.

One of the meekest characters in history was John the Baptist. You remember when they sent a deputation to him and asked if he was Elias, or this prophet, or that prophet, he said, "No." Now he might have said some very flattering things of himself. He might have said:

"I am the son of the old priest Zacharias. Haven't you heard of my fame as a preacher? I have baptized more people probably, than any man living. The world has never seen a preacher like myself."

I honestly believe that in the present day most men standing in his position would do that. On the railroad train, some time ago, I heard a man talking so loud that all the people in the car could hear him. He said that he had baptized more people than any man in his denomination. He told how many thousand miles he had traveled, how many sermons he had preached, how many open-air services he had held, and this and that, until I was so ashamed that I had to hide my head. This is the age of boasting. It is the day of the great "I."

My attention was recently called to the fact that in all the Psalms you cannot find any place where David refers to his victory over the giant, Goliath. If it had been in the present day, there would have been a volume written about it at once; I don't know how many poems there would be telling of the great things that this man had done. He would have been in demand as a lecturer, and would have added a title to his name: G. G. K.,—Great Giant Killer. That is how it is to-day: great evangelists, great preachers, great theologians, great bishops.

"John," they asked, "who are you?"

"I am nobody. I am to be heard, not to be seen. I am only a voice."

He hadn't a word to say about himself. I once heard a little bird faintly singing close by me,—at last it got clear out of sight, and then its notes were still sweeter. The higher it flew the sweeter sounded its notes. If we can only get self out of sight and learn of Him who was meek and lowly in heart we shall be lifted up into heavenly places.

Mark tells us, in the first chapter and seventh verse, that John came and preached saying, "There cometh one mightier than I after me, the latchet of whose shoes I am not worthy to stoop down and unloose." Think of that; and bear in mind that Christ was looked upon as a deceiver, a village carpenter, and yet here is John, the son of the old priest, who had a much higher position in the sight of men than that of Jesus. Great crowds were coming to hear him, and even Herod attended his meetings.

When his disciples came and told John that Christ was beginning to draw crowds, he nobly answered: "A man can receive nothing, except it be given him from heaven. Ye yourselves bear me witness that I said, I am not the Christ, but that I am sent before Him. He that hath the bride is the bridegroom: but the friend of the bridegroom, which standeth and heareth him, rejoiceth greatly because of the bridegroom's voice: this my joy therefore is fulfilled. He must increase, but I must decrease."

It is easy to read that, but it is hard for us to live in the power of it. It is very hard for us to be ready to decrease, to grow smaller and smaller, that Christ may increase. The morning star fades away when the sun rises.

"He that cometh from above is above all: he that is of the earth is earthly, and speaketh of the earth: He that cometh from heaven is above all, and what He hath seen and heard, that He testifieth; and no man receiveth His testimony. He that hath received His testimony hath set to his seal that God is true. For He whom God hath sent speaketh the words of God: for God giveth not the Spirit by measure unto Him."

Let us now turn the light upon ourselves. Have we been decreasing of late? Do we think less of ourselves and of our position than we did a year ago? Are we seeking to obtain some position of dignity? Are we wanting to hold on to some title, and are we offended because we are not treated with the courtesy that we think is due us? Some time ago I heard a man in the pulpit say that he should take offence if he was not addressed by his title. My dear friend, are you

going to take that position that you must have a title, and
that you must have every letter addressed with that title or
you will be offended? John did not want any title, and when
we are right with God, we shall not be caring about titles.
In one of his early epistles Paul calls himself the "least of
all the apostles." Later on he claims to be "less than the
least of all saints," and again, just before his death, humbly
declares that he is the "chief of sinners." Notice how he
seems to have grown smaller and smaller in his own
estimation. So it was with John. And I do hope and pray
that as the days go by we may feel like hiding ourselves,
and let God have all the honor and glory.

"When I look back upon my own religious experience,"
says Andrew Murray, "or round upon the Church of Christ
in the world, I stand amazed at the thought of how little
humility is sought after as the distinguishing feature of the
discipleship of Jesus. In preaching and living, in the daily
intercourse of the home and social life, in the more special
fellowship with Christians, in the direction and
performance of work for Christ—alas! how much proof
there is that humility is not esteemed the cardinal virtue,
the only root from which the graces can grow, the one
indispensable condition of true fellowship with Jesus."

See what Christ says about John. "He was a burning and
shining light." Christ gave him the honor that belonged to
him. If you take a humble position, Christ will see it. If you
want God to help you, then take a low position.

I am afraid that if we had been in John's place, many of us
would have said: "What did Christ say,—I am a burning
and shining light?" Then we would have had that
recommendation put in the newspapers, and would have
sent them to our friends, with that part marked in blue

pencil. Sometimes I get a letter just full of clippings from the newspapers, stating that this man is more eloquent than Gough, etc. And the man wants me to get him some church. Do you think that a man who has such eloquence would be looking for a church? No, they would all be looking for him.

My dear friends, isn't it humiliating? Sometimes I think it is a wonder that any man is converted these days. Let another praise you. Don't be around praising yourself. If we want God to lift us up, let us get down. The lower we get, the higher God will lift us. It is Christ's eulogy of John, "Greater than any man born of woman."

There is a story told of Carey, the great missionary, that he was invited by the Governor-general of India to go to a dinner party at which were some military officers belonging to the aristocracy, and who looked down upon missionaries with scorn and contempt.

One of these officers said at the table: "I believe that Carey was a shoemaker, wasn't he, before he took up the profession of a missionary?"

Mr. Carey spoke up and said: "Oh no, I was only a cobbler. I could mend shoes, and wasn't ashamed of it."

The one prominent virtue of Christ, next to His obedience, is His humility; and even His obedience grew out of His humility. Being in the form of God, He counted it not a thing to be grasped to be on an equality with God, but He emptied Himself, taking the form of a bond-servant, and was made in the likeness of men. And being found in fashion as a man, He humbled Himself, and became obedient unto death, yea, the death of the cross. In His lowly birth, His submission to His earthly parents, His seclusion during thirty years, His consorting with the poor and despised, His entire submission and dependence upon His Father, this virtue that was consummated in His death on the cross, shines out.

One day Jesus was on His way to Capernaum, and was talking about His coming death and suffering, and about His resurrection, and He heard quite a heated discussion going on behind Him. When He came into the house at Capernaum, He turned to His disciples, and said:

"What was all that discussion about?"

I see John look at James, and Peter at Andrew,—and they all looked ashamed. "Who shall be the greater?" That discussion has wrecked party after party, one society after another—"Who shall be the greatest?"

The way Christ took to teach them humility was by putting a little child in their midst and saying: "If you want to be great, take that little child for an example, and he who wants to be the greatest, let him be servant of all."

To me, one of the saddest things in all the life of Jesus Christ was the fact that just before His crucifixion, His disciples should have been striving to see who should be the greatest, that night He instituted the Supper, and they ate the Passover together. It was His last night on earth, and they never saw Him so sorrowful before. He knew Judas was going to sell Him for thirty pieces of silver. He knew that Peter would deny Him. And yet, in addition to this, when going into the very shadow of the cross, there arose this strife as to who should be the greatest. He took a towel and girded Himself like a slave, and He took a basin of water and stooped and washed their feet. That was another object lesson of humility. He said, "Ye call me Lord, and ye do well. If you want to be great in my Kingdom, be servant of all. If you serve, you shall be great."

When the Holy Ghost came, and those men were filled, from that time on mark the difference: Matthew takes up his pen to write, and he keeps Matthew out of sight. He tells what Peter and Andrew did, but he calls himself Matthew "the publican." He tells how they left all to follow Christ, but does not mention the feast he gave. Jerome says that Mark's gospel is to be regarded as memoirs of Peter's discourses, and to have been published by his authority. Yet here we constantly find that damaging things are mentioned about Peter, and things to his credit are not referred to. Mark's gospel omits all allusion to Peter's faith in venturing on the sea, but goes into detail about the story of his fall and denial of our Lord. Peter put himself down, and lifted others up.

If the Gospel of Luke had been written to-day, it would be signed by the great Dr. Luke, and you would have his photograph as a frontispiece. But you can't find Luke's name; he keeps out of sight. He wrote two books, and his name is not to be found in either. John covers himself always under the expression—"the disciple whom Jesus loved." None of the four men whom history and tradition assert to be the authors of the gospels, lay claim to the authorship in their writings. Dear man of God, I would that I had the same spirit, that I could just get out of sight,— hide myself.

My dear friends, I believe our only hope is to be filled with the Spirit of Christ. May God fill us, so that we shall be filled with meekness and humility. Let us take the hymn,

"O, to be nothing, nothing," and make it the language of our hearts. It breathes the spirit of Him who said: "The Son can do nothing of Himself!"

Oh to be nothing, nothing!

Only to lie at His feet,

A broken and emptied vessel,

For the Master's use made meet.

Emptied, that He might fill me

As forth to His service I go;

Broken, that so unhindered,

His life through me might flow.

REST.

Some years ago a gentleman came to me and asked me
which I thought was the most precious promise of all those
that Christ left. I took some time to look them over, but I
gave it up. I found that I could not answer the question. It is
like a man with a large family of children, he cannot tell
which he likes best; he loves them all. But if not the best,
this is one of the sweetest promises of all: "Come unto Me,
all ye that labor and are heavy laden, and I will give you
rest. Take my yoke upon you, and learn of Me, for I am
meek and lowly in heart: and ye shall find rest unto your
souls. For my yoke is easy, and My burden is light."

There are a good many people who think the promises are
not going to be fulfilled. There are some that you do see
fulfilled, and you cannot help but believe they are true.
Now remember that all the promises are not given without
conditions. Some are given with, and others without,
conditions attached to them. For instance, it says, "If I
regard iniquity in my heart, the Lord will not hear me."
Now, I need not pray as long as I am cherishing some
known sin. He will not hear me, much less answer me. The
Lord says in the eighty fourth Psalm, "No good thing will
he withhold from them that walk uprightly." If I am not
walking uprightly I have no claims under the promise.
Again, some of the promises were made to certain
individuals or nations. For instance, God said that He
would make Abraham's seed to multiply as the stars of
heaven: but that is not a promise for you or me. Some
promises were made to the Jews, and do not apply to the
Gentiles.

Then there are promises without conditions. He promised Adam and Eve that the world should have a Savior, and there was no power in earth or perdition that could keep Christ from coming at the appointed time. When Christ left the world, He said He would send us the Holy Ghost. He had only been gone ten days when the Holy Ghost came. And so you can run right through the Scriptures, and you will find that some of the promises are with, and some without, conditions; and if we don't comply with the conditions we cannot expect them to be fulfilled.

I believe it will be the experience of every man and woman on the face of the earth, I believe that everyone will be obliged to testify in the evening of life, that if they have complied with the condition, the Lord has fulfilled His word to the letter. Joshua, the old Hebrew hero, was an illustration. After having tested God forty years in the Egyptian brick-kilns, forty years in the desert, and thirty years in the Promised Land, his dying testimony was: "Not one thing hath failed of all the good things which the Lord promised." I believe you could heave the ocean easier than break one of God's promises. So when we come to a promise like the one we have before us now, I want you to bear in mind that there is no discount upon it. "Come unto Me, all ye that labor and are heavy laden, and I will give you rest."

Perhaps you say: "I hope Mr. Moody is not going to preach on this old text." Yes: I am. When I take up an album, it does not interest me if all the photographs are new; but if I know any of the faces. I stop at once. So with these old, well-known texts. They have quenched our thirst before, but the water is still bubbling up—we cannot drink it dry.

If you probe the human heart, you will find a want, and that want is rest. The cry of the world to day is, "Where can rest be found?" Why are theaters and places of amusement crowded at night? What is the secret of Sunday driving, of the saloons and brothels? Some think they are going to get it in pleasure, others think they are going to get it in wealth, and others in literature. They are seeking and finding no rest.

Where Can Rest be Found?

If I wanted to find a person who had rest I would not go among the very wealthy. The man that we read of in the twelfth chapter of Luke, thought he was going to get rest by multiplying his goods, but he was disappointed. "Soul, take thine ease." I venture to say that there is not a person in this wide world who has tried to find rest in that way and found it.

Money cannot buy it. Many a millionaire would gladly give millions if he could purchase it as he does his stocks and shares. God has made the soul a little too large for this world. Roll the whole world in, and still there is room. There is care in getting wealth, and more care in keeping it.

Nor would I go among the pleasure seekers. They have a few hours' enjoyment, but the next day there is enough sorrow to counterbalance it. They may drink the cup of pleasure to-day, but the cup of pain comes on to-morrow.

To find rest I would never go among the politicians, or among the so-called great. Congress is the last place on earth that I would go. In the Lower House they want to go to the Senate; in the Senate they want to go to the Cabinet; and then they want to go to the White House; and rest has never been found there. Nor would I go among the halls of learning. "Much study is a weariness to the flesh." I would not go among the upper ten, the "bon-ton," for they are constantly chasing after fashion. Have you not noticed their troubled faces on our streets? And the face is index to the soul. They have no hopeful look. Their worship of pleasure is slavery. Solomon tried pleasure, and found bitter disappointment, and down the ages has come the bitter cry, "All is vanity."

Now, there is no rest in sin. The wicked know nothing about it. The Scriptures tell us the wicked "are like the troubled sea that cannot rest." You have, perhaps been on the sea when there is a calm, when the water is as clear as crystal, and it seemed as if the sea were at rest. But if you looked you would see that the waves came in, and that the calm was only on the surface. Man, like the sea, has no rest. He has had no rest since Adam fell, and there is none for him until he returns to God again, and the light of Christ shines into his heart.

Rest cannot be found in the world, and thank God the world cannot take it from the believing heart! Sin is the cause of all this unrest. It brought toil and labor and misery into the world.

Now for something positive. I would go successfully to someone who has heard the sweet voice of Jesus, and has laid his burden down at the cross. There is rest, sweet rest. Thousands could certify to this blessed fact. They could say, and truthfully:

I heard the voice of Jesus say,

"Come unto me and rest.

Lay down, thou weary one, lay down,

Thy head upon my breast."

I came to Jesus as I was,

Weary and worn and sad.

I found in Him a resting-place,

And He hath made me glad.

Among all his writings St. Augustine has nothing sweeter than this: "Thou hast made us for Thyself, O God, and our heart is restless till it rests in Thee."

Do you know that for four thousand years no prophet or priest or patriarch ever stood up and uttered a text like this? It would be blasphemy for Moses to have uttered a text like it. Do you think he had rest when he was teasing the Lord to let him go into the Promised Land? Do you think Elijah could have uttered such a text as this, when, under the juniper-tree, he prayed that he might die? And this is one of the strongest proofs that Jesus Christ was not only man, but God. He was God-Man, and this is Heaven's proclamation, "Come unto Me, and I will give you rest". He brought it down from heaven with Him.

Now, if this text was not true, don't you think it would have been found out by this time? I believe it as much as I believe in my existence. Why? Because I not only find it in the Book, but in my own experience. The "I wills" of Christ have never been broken, and never can be.

I thank God for the word "give" in that passage. He doesn't
sell it. Some of us are so poor that we could not buy it if it
was for sale. Thank God, we can get it for nothing.

I like to have a text like this, because it takes us all in.
"Come unto me all ye that labor." That doesn't mean a
select few—refined ladies and cultured men. It doesn't
mean good people only. It applies to saint and sinner.
Hospitals are for the sick, not for healthy people. Do you
think that Christ would shut the door in anyone's face, and
say, "I did not mean all; I only meant certain ones"? If you
cannot come as a saint, come as a sinner. Only come!

A lady told me once that she was so hard-hearted she
couldn't come.

"Well," I said, "my good woman, it doesn't say all ye soft-
hearted people come. Black hearts, vile hearts, hard hearts,
soft hearts, all hearts come. Who can soften your hard heart
but Himself?"

The harder the heart, the more need you have to come. If
my watch stops I don't take it to a drug store or to a
blacksmith's shop, but to the watchmaker's, to have it
repaired. So if the heart gets out of order take it to its
keeper, Christ, to have it set right. If you can prove that you
are a sinner, you are entitled to the promise. Get all the
benefit you can out of it.

Now, there are a good many believers who think this text
applies only to sinners; It is just the thing for them too.
What do we see to-day? The Church, Christian people, all
loaded down with cares and troubles. "Come unto me all ye
that labor." All! I believe that includes the Christian whose

heart is burdened with some great sorrow. The Lord wants you to come.

Christ the Burden-Bearer.

It says in another place, "Casting all your care upon Him, for He careth for you." We would have a victorious Church if we could get Christian people to realize that. But they have never made the discovery. They agree that Christ is the sin-bearer, but they do not realize that He is also the burden-bearer. "Surely He hath borne our griefs and carried our sorrows." It is the privilege of every child of God to walk in unclouded sunlight.

Some people go back into the past and rake up all the troubles they ever had, and then they look into the future and anticipate that they will have still more trouble, and they go reeling and staggering all through life. They give you the cold chills every time they meet you. They put on a whining voice, and tell you what "a hard time they have had." I believe they embalm them, and bring out the mummy on every opportunity. The Lord says, "Cast all your care on Me. I want to carry your burdens and your troubles." What we want is a joyful Church, and we are not going to convert the world until we have it. We want to get this long-faced Christianity off the face of the earth.

Take these people that have some great burden, and let them come into a meeting. If you can get their attention upon the singing or preaching, they will say, "Oh, wasn't it grand! I forgot all my cares." And they just drop their bundle at the end of the pew. But the moment the benediction is pronounced they grab the bundle again. You laugh, but you do it yourself. Cast your care on Him.

Sometimes they go into their closet and close their door, and they get so carried away and lifted up that they forget their trouble; but they just take it up again the moment they get off their knees. Leave your sorrow now; cast all your care upon Him. If you cannot come to Christ as a saint, come as a sinner. But if you are a saint with some trouble or care, bring it to Him. Saint and sinner, come! He wants you all. Don't let Satan deceive you into believing that you cannot come if you will. Christ says, "Ye will not come unto Me." With the command comes the power.

A man in one of our meetings in Europe said he would like to come, but he was chained, and couldn't come.

A Scotchman said to him, "Ay, man, why don't you come chain and all?"

He said, "I never thought of that."

Are you cross and peevish, and do you make things unpleasant at home? My friend, come to Christ and ask Him to help you. Whatever the sin is, bring it to Him.

What Does it Mean to Come?

Perhaps you say, "Mr. Moody, I wish you would tell us what it is to come." I have given up trying to explain it. I always feel like the colored minister who said he was going to confound, instead of expound, the chapter.

The best definition is just—come. The more you try to explain it, the more you are mystified. About the first thing a mother teaches her child is to look. She takes the baby to the window, and says, "Look, baby, papa is coming!" Then she teaches the child to come. She props it up against a chair, and says, "Come!" and by and by the little thing pushes the chair along towards mamma. That's coming. You don't need to go to college to learn how. You don't need any minister to tell you what it is. Now will you come to Christ? He said, "Him that cometh unto Me, I will in no wise cast out."

When we have such a promise as this, let us cling to it, and never give it up. Christ is not mocking us. He wants us to come with all our sins and backslidings, and throw ourselves upon His bosom. It is our sins God wants, not our tears only. They alone do no good. And we cannot come through resolutions. Action is necessary. How many times at church have we said, "I will turn over a new leaf," but the Monday leaf is worse than the Saturday leaf.

The way to heaven is straight as a rule, but it is the way of the cross. Don't try to get around it. Shall I tell you what the "yoke" referred to in the text is? It is the cross which Christians must bear. The only way by which you can find rest in this dark world is by taking up the yoke of Christ. I do not know what it may include in your case, beyond taking up your Christian duties, acknowledging Christ and acting as becomes one of His disciples. Perhaps it may be to erect a gamily altar; or to tell a godless husband that you have made up your mind to serve God; or to tell your parents that you want to be a Christian. Follow the will of God, and happiness and peace and rest will come. The way of obedience is always the way of blessing.

I was preaching in Chicago to a hall full of women one Sunday afternoon, and after the meeting was over a lady came to me and said she wanted to talk to me. She said she would accept Christ, and after some conversation she went home. I looked for her for a whole week, but didn't see her until the following Sunday afternoon. She came and sat down right in front of me, and her face had such a sad expression. She seemed to have entered into the misery, instead of the joy, of the Lord.

After the meeting was over I went to her and asked her what the trouble was.

She said: "Oh, Mr. Moody, this has been the most miserable week of my life."

I asked her if there was anyone with whom she had had trouble and whom she could not forgive.

She said: "No, not that I know of."

"Well, did you tell your friends about having found the Savior?"

"Indeed I didn't, I have been all the week trying to keep it from them."

"Well," I said, "that is the reason why you have no peace."

She wanted to take the crown, but did not want the cross. My friends, you must go by the way of Calvary. If you ever get rest, you must get it at the foot of the cross.

"Why," she said, "if I should go home and tell my infidel husband that I had found Christ I don't know what he would do. I think he would turn me out."

"Well," I said, "go out."

She went away, promising that she would tell him, timid and pale, but she did not want another wretched week. She was bound to have peace.

The next night I gave a lecture to men only, and in the hall there were eight thousand men and one solitary woman. When I got through and went into the inquiry meeting, I found this lady with her husband. She introduced him to me (he was a doctor, and a very influential man) and said:

"He wants to become a Christian."

I took my Bible and told him all about Christ, and he accepted Him. I said to her after it was all over:

"It turned out quite differently from what you expected, didn't it?"

"Yes," she replied, "I was never so scared in my life. I expected he would do something dreadful, but it has turned out so well."

She took God's way, and got rest.

I want to say to young ladies, perhaps you have a godless father or mother, a sceptical brother, who is going down through drink, and perhaps there is no one who can reach them but you. How many times a godly, pure young lady has taken the light into some darkened home! Many a home might be lit up with the Gospel if the mothers and daughters would only speak the word.

The last time Mr. Sankey and myself were in Edinburgh, there were a father, two sisters and a brother, who used every morning to take the morning paper and pick my sermon to pieces. They were indignant to think that the Edinburgh people should be carried away with such preaching. One day one of the sisters was going by the hall, and she thought she would drop in and see what class of people went there. She happened to take a seat by a godly lady, who said to her:

"I hope you are interested in this work."

She tossed her head and said: "Indeed I am not. I am disgusted with everything I have seen and heard."

"Well," said the lady, "perhaps you came prejudiced."

"Yes, and the meeting has not removed any of it, but has rather increased it."

"I have received a great deal of good from them."

"There is nothing here for me. I don't see how an intellectual person can be interested."

To make a long story short, she got the lady to promise to come back. When the meeting broke up, just a little of the prejudice had worn away. She promised to come back again the next day, and then she attended three or four more meetings, and became quite interested. She said nothing to her family, until finally the burden became too heavy, and she told them. They laughed at her, and made her the butt of their ridicule.

One day the two sisters were together, and the other said: "Now what have you got at those meetings that you didn't have in the first place?"

"I have a peace that I never knew of before. I am at peace with God, myself and all the world." Did you ever have a little war of your own with your neighbors, in your own family? And she said: "I have self-control. You know, sister, if you had said half the mean things before I was converted that you have said since, I would have been angry and answered back, but if you remember correctly, I haven't answered once since I have been converted."

The sister said: "You certainly have something that I have not." The other told her it was for her too, and she brought the sister to the meetings, where she found peace.

Like Martha and Mary, they had a brother, but he was a member of the University of Edinburgh. He be converted? He go to these meetings? It might do for women, but not for him. One night they came home and told him that a chum of his own, a member of the University, had stood up and confessed Christ, and when he sat down his brother got up and confessed; and so with the third one.

When the young man heard it, he said: "Do you mean to tell me that he has been converted?"

"Yes."

"Well," he said, "there must be something in it."

He put on his hat, and coat, and went to see his friend Black. Black got him down to the meetings, and he was converted.

We went through to Glasgow, and had not been there six weeks when news came that that young man had been stricken down and died. When he was dying he called his father to his bedside and said:

"Wasn't it a good thing that my sisters went to those meetings? Won't you meet me in heaven, father?"

"Yes, my son, I am so glad you are a Christian; that is the only comfort that I have in losing you. I will become a Christian, and will meet you again."

I tell this to encourage some sister to go home and carry the message of salvation. It may be that your brother may be taken away in a few months. My dear friends, are we not living in solemn days? Isn't it time for us to get our friends into the Kingdom of God? Come, wife, won't you tell your husband? Come, sister, won't you tell your brother? Won't you take up your cross now? The blessing of God will rest on your soul if you will.

I was in Wales once, and a lady told me this little story: An English friend of hers, a mother, had a child that was sick. At first they considered there was no danger, until one day the doctor came in and said that the symptoms were very unfavorable. He took the mother out of the room, and told her that the child could not live. It came like a thunderbolt. After the doctor had gone the mother went into the room where the child lay and began to talk to the child and tried to divert its mind.

"Darling, do you know you will soon hear the music of heaven? You will hear a sweeter song than you have ever heard on earth. You will hear them sing the song of Moses and the Lamb. You are very fond of music. Won't it be sweet, darling?"

And the little tired, sick child turned its head away, and said, "Oh mamma, I am so tired and so sick that I think it would make me worse to hear all that music."

"Well," the mother said, "you will soon see Jesus, You will see the seraphim and cherubim and the streets all paved with gold"; and she went on picturing heaven as it is described in Revelation.

The little tired child again turned its head away, and said, "Oh mamma, I am so tired that I think it would make me worse to see all those beautiful things!"

At last the mother took the child up in her arms, and pressed her to her loving heart. And the little sick one whispered:

"Oh mamma, that is what I want. If Jesus will only take me in His arms and let me rest!"

Dear friend, are you not tired and weary of sin? Are you not weary of the turmoil of life? You can end rest on the bosom of the Son of God.

SEVEN "I WILLS" OF CHRIST.

A man when he says "I will," may not mean much. We very often say "I will," when we don't mean to fulfil what we say; but when we come to the "I will" of Christ, He means to fulfil it. Everything He has promised to do, He is able and willing to accomplish; and He is going to do it. I cannot find any passage in Scripture in which He says "I will" do this, or "I will" do that, but it will be done.

1. The "I Will" of Salvation.

The first "I will" to which I want to direct your attention, is to be found in John's gospel, sixth chapter and thirty-seventh verse: "Him that cometh unto Me I will in no wise cast out."

I imagine someone will say, "Well, if I was what I ought to be, I would come; but when my mind goes over the past record of my life, it is too dark. I am not fit to come."

You must bear in mind that Jesus Christ came to save not good people, not the upright and just, but sinners like you and me, who have gone astray, and sinned and come short of the glory of God. Listen to this "I will"—it goes right into the heart—"Him that cometh unto Me, I will in no wise cast out." Surely that is broad enough—is it not? I don't care who the man or woman is; I don't care what their trials, what their troubles, what their sorrows, or what their sins are, if they will only come straight to the Master,

He will not cast them out. Come then, poor sinner; come just as you are, and take Him at His word.

He is so anxious to save sinners, He will take everyone who comes. He will take those who are so full of sin that they are despised by all who know them, who have been rejected by their fathers and mothers, who have been cast off by the wives of their bosoms. He will take those who have sunk so low that upon them no eye of pity is cast. His occupation is to hear and save. That is what He left heaven and came into the world for; that is what He left the throne of God for—to save sinners. "The Son of man is come to seek and to save that which was lost." He did not come to condemn the world but that the world through Him might be saved.

A wild and prodigal young man, who was running a headlong career to ruin came into one of our meetings in Chicago. The Spirit of God got hold of him. Whilst I was conversing with him, and endeavoring to bring him to Christ, I quoted this verse to him.

I asked him: "Do you believe Christ said that?"

"I suppose He did."

"Suppose He did! do you believe it?"

"I hope so."

"Hope so! do you believe it? You do your work, and the Lord will do His. Just come as you are, and throw yourself upon His bosom, and He will not cast you out."

This man thought it was too simple and easy.

At last light seemed to break in upon him, and he seemed to find comfort from it. It was past midnight before he got down on his knees, but down he went, and was converted. I said:

"Now, don't think you are going to get out of the devil's territory without trouble. The devil will come to you to-morrow morning, and say it was all feeling; that you only imagined you were accepted by God. When he does, don't fight him with your own opinions, but fight him with John 6:37: 'Him that cometh to Me I will in no wise cast out.' Let that be the 'sword of the Spirit.'"

I don't believe that any man ever starts to go to Christ, but the devil strives somehow or other to meet him and trip him up. And even after he has come to Christ, the devil tries to assail him with doubts, and make him believe there is something wrong in it.

The struggle came sooner than I thought in this man's case. When he was on his way home the devil assailed him. He used this text, but the devil put this thought into his mind: "How do you know Christ ever said that after all? Perhaps the translators made a mistake."

Into darkness he went again. He was in trouble till about two in the morning. At last he came to this conclusion. Said he:

"I will believe it anyway; and when I get to heaven, if it isn't true, I will just tell the Lord I didn't make the mistake—the translators made it."

The kings and princes of this world, when they issue invitations, call round them the rich, the mighty and powerful, the honorable and the wise; but the Lord, when He was on earth; called round Him the vilest of the vile. That was the principal fault the people found with Him. Those self-righteous Pharisees were not going to associate with harlots and publicans. The principal charge against Him was: "This man receiveth sinners and eateth with them." Who would have such a man around him as John Bunyan in his time? He, a Bedford tinker, couldn't get inside one of the princely castles. I was very much amused when I was over on the other side. They had erected a monument to John Bunyan, and it was unveiled by lords and dukes and great men. While he was on earth, they would not have allowed him inside the walls of their castles. Yet he was made one of the mightiest instruments in the spread of the Gospel. No book that has ever been written comes so near the Bible as John Bunyan's "Pilgrim's Progress." And he was a poor Bedford tinker. So it is with God. He picks up some poor, lost tramp, and makes him an instrument to turn hundreds and thousands to Christ.

George Whitefield, standing in his tabernacle in London, and with a multitude gathered about him, cried out: "The Lord Jesus will save the devil's castaways!"

Two poor abandoned wretches standing outside in the street, heard him, as his silvery voice rang out on the air. Looking into each other's faces, they said: "That must mean you and me." They wept and rejoiced. They drew near and looked in at the door, at the face of the earnest messenger, the tears streaming from his eyes as he plead with the people to give their hearts to God. One of them wrote him a little note and sent it to him.

Later that day, as he sat at the table of Lady Huntington, who was his special friend, someone present said:

"Mr. Whitefield, did you not go a little too far to-day when you said that the Lord would save the devil's castaways?"

Taking the note from his pocket he gave it to the lady, and said: "Will you read that note aloud?"

She read: "Mr. Whitefield: Two poor lost women stood outside your tabernacle to-day, and heard you say that the Lord would save the devil's castaways. We seized upon that as our last hope, and we write you this to tell you that we rejoice now in believing in Him, and from this good hour we shall endeavor to serve Him, who has done so much for us."

2. The "I Will" of Cleansing.

The next "I will" is found in Luke, fifth chapter. We read of a leper who came to Christ, and said: "Lord, if Thou wilt, Thou canst make me clean." The Lord touched him, saying, "I will: be thou clean"; and immediately the leprosy left him.

Now if any man or woman full of the leprosy of sin read this, if you will but go to the Master and tell all your case to Him, He will speak to you as He did to that poor leper and say. "I will: be thou clean," and the leprosy of your sins will flee away from you. It is the Lord, and the Lord alone, who can forgive sins. If you say to Him, "Lord, I am full of sin; Thou canst make me clean"; "Lord, I have a terrible temper; Thou canst make me clean"; "Lord, I have a deceitful heart. Cleanse me, O Lord; give me a new heart. O Lord, give me the power to overcome the flesh, and the snares of the devil!"; "Lord, I am full of unclean habits"; if you come to Him with a sincere spirit, you will hear the voice, "I will; be thou clean." It will be done. Do you think that the God who created the world out of nothing, who by a breath put life into the world—do you think that if He says, "Thou shalt be clean," you will not?

Now, you can make a wonderful exchange to-day. You can have health in the place of sickness; you can get rid of everything that is vile and hateful in the sight of God. The Son of God comes down, and says, "I will take away your leprosy, and give you health in its stead. I will take away that terrible disease that is ruining your body and soul, and give you my righteousness in its stead. I will clothe you with the garments of salvation."

Is it not wonderful? That's what He means when He says— I will. Oh, lay hold of this "I will!"

3. The "I Will" of Confession.

Now turn to Matthew, tenth chapter, thirty-second verse: "Whosoever therefore shall confess Me before men, him will I confess also before my Father which is in heaven." There's the "I will" of confession.

Now, that's the next thing that takes place after a man is saved. When we have been washed in the blood of the Lamb, the next thing is to get our mouths opened. We have to confess Christ here in this dark world, and tell His love to others. We are not to be ashamed of the Son of God.

A man thinks it a great honor when he has achieved a
victory that causes his name to be mentioned in the English
Parliament, or in the presence of the Queen and her court.
How excited we used to be during the war, when some
general did something extraordinary, and someone got up
in Congress to confess his exploits; how the papers used to
talk about it! In China, we read, the highest ambition of the
successful soldier is to have his name written in the palace
or temple of Confucius. But just think of having your name
mentioned in the kingdom of heaven by the Prince of
Glory, by the Son of God, because you confess Him here
on earth! You confess Him here; He will confess you
yonder.

If you wish to be brought into the clear light of liberty, you
must take your stand on Christ's side. I have known many
Christians go groping about in darkness, and never get into
the clear light of the kingdom, because they were ashamed
to confess the Son of God. We are living in a day when
men want a religion without the cross. They want the
crown, but not the cross. But if we are to be disciples of
Jesus Christ, we have to take up our crosses daily—not
once a year, or on the Sabbath, but daily. And if we take up
our crosses and follow Him, we shall be blessed in the very
act.

I remember a man in New York who used to come and pray
with me. He had his cross. He was afraid to confess Christ.
It seemed that down at the bottom of his trunk he had a
Bible. He wanted to get it out and read it to the companion
with whom he lived, but he was ashamed to do it. For a
whole week that was his cross; and after he had carried the
burden that long, and after a terrible struggle, he made up
his mind. He said, "I will take my Bible out tonight and

read it." He took it out, and soon he heard the footsteps of his mate coming upstairs.

His first impulse was to put it away again, but then he thought he would not—he would face his companion with it. His mate came in, and seeing him at his Bible, said,

"John, are you interested in these things?" "Yes," he replied.

"How long has this been, then?" asked his companion.

"Exactly a week," he answered; "for a whole week I have tried to get out my Bible to read to you, but I have never done so till now."

"Well," said his friend, "it is a strange thing. I was converted on the some night, and I too was ashamed to take my Bible out."

You are ashamed to take your Bible out and say, "I have lived a godless life for all these years, but I will commence now to live a life of righteousness." You are ashamed to open your Bible and read that blessed Psalm, "The Lord is my Shepherd, I shall not want." You are ashamed to be seen on your knees. No man can be a disciple of Jesus Christ without bearing His cross. A great many people want to know how it is Jesus Christ has so few disciples, whilst Mahomet has so many. The reason is that Mahomet gives no cross to bear. There are so few men who will come out to take their stand.

I was struck during the American war with the fact that there were so many men who could go to the cannon's mouth without trembling, but who had not courage to take up their Bibles to read them at night. They were ashamed of the Gospel of Jesus Christ, which is the power of God unto salvation. "Whosoever therefore shall confess me before men, him will I confess also before My Father which is in heaven. But whosoever shall deny Me before men, him will I also deny before My Father which is in heaven."

4. The "I Will" of Service.

The next I will is the "I will" of service.

There are a good many Christians who have been quickened and aroused to say, "I want to do some service for Christ."

Well, Christ says, "Follow Me, and I will make you fishers of men."

There is no Christian who cannot help to bring someone to the Savior. Christ says, "And I, if I be lifted up, will draw all men unto Me"; and our business is just to lift up Christ.

Our Lord said, "Follow Me, Peter, and I will make you a fisher of men"; and Peter simply obeyed Him, and there, on that day of Pentecost, we see the result. Peter had a good haul on the day of Pentecost. I doubt if he ever caught so many fish in one day as he did men on that day. It would have broken every net they had on board, if they had had to drag up three thousand fishes.

I read some time ago of a man who took passage in a stage coach. There were first, second and third-class passengers. But when he looked into the coach, he saw all the passengers sitting together without distinction. He could not understand it till by-and-by they came to a hill, and the coach stopped, and the driver called out, "First-class passengers keep their seats, second-class passengers get out and walk, third class passengers get behind and push." Now in the Church we have no room for first-class passengers—people who think that salvation means an easy ride all the way to heaven. We have no room for second class passengers—people who are carried most of the time, and who, when they must work out their own salvation, go trudging on giving never a thought to helping their fellows along. All church members ought to be third class passengers—ready to dismount and push all together, and push with a will. That was John Wesley's definition of a church—"All at it, and always at it." Every Christian ought to be a worker. He need not be a preacher, he need not be an evangelist, to be useful. He may be useful in business. See what power an employer has, if he likes! How he could labor with his employees, and in his business relations! Often a man can be far more useful in a business sphere than he could in another.

There is one reason, and a great reason, why so many do not succeed. I have been asked by a great many good men, "Why is it we don't have any results? We work hard, pray hard, and preach hard, and yet the success does not come." I will tell you. It is because they spend all their time mending their nets. No wonder they never catch anything.

The great matter is to hold inquiry meetings, and thus pull the net in, and see if you have caught anything. If you are always mending and setting the net, you won't catch many fish. Whoever heard of a man going out to fish, and setting his net, and then letting it stop there, and never pulling it in? Everybody would laugh at the man's folly.

A minister in England came to me one day, and said, "I wish you would tell me why we ministers don't succeed better than we do."

I brought before him this idea of pulling in the net, and I said, "You ought to pull in your nets. There are many ministers in Manchester who can preach much better than I can, but I pull in the net."

Many people have objections to inquiry meetings, but I urged upon him the importance of them, and the minister said,

"I never did pull in my net, but I will try next Sunday."

He did so, and eight persons, anxious inquirers, went into his study. The next Sunday he came down to see me, and said he had never had such a Sunday in his life. He had met with marvelous blessing. The next time he drew the net there were forty, and when he came to see me later, he said to me joyfully,

"Moody, I have had eight hundred conversions this last year! It is a great mistake I did not begin earlier to pull in the net."

So, my friends, if you want to catch men, just pull in the net. If you only catch one, it will be something. It may be a little child, but I have known a little child to convert a whole family. You don't know what is in that little dull-headed boy in the inquiry-room; he may become a Martin Luther, a reformer that shall make the world tremble—you cannot tell. God uses the weak things of this world to confound the mighty. God's promise is as good as a bank note—"I promise to pay So-and-So," and here is one of

Christ's promissory notes—"If you follow Me, I will make you fishers of men." Will you not lay hold of the promise, and trust it, and follow Him now?

If a man preaches the Gospel, and preaches it faithfully, he ought to expect results then and there. I believe it is the privilege of God's children to reap the fruit of their labor three hundred and sixty five days in the year.

"Well, but," say some, "is there not a sowing time as well as harvest?"

Yes, it is true, there is; but then, you can sow with one hand, and reap with the other. What would you think of a farmer who went on sowing all the year round, and never thought of reaping? I repeat it, we want to sow with one hand, and reap with the other; and if we look for the fruit of our labors, we shall see it. "I, if I be lifted up, will draw all men unto Me." We must lift Christ up, and then seek men out, and bring them to Him.

You must use the right kind of bait. A good many don't do this, and then they wonder they are not successful. You see them getting up all kinds of entertainments with which to try and catch men. They go the wrong way to work. This perishing world wants Christ, and Him crucified. There's a void in every man's bosom that wants filling up, and if we only approach him with the right kind of bait, we shall catch him. This poor world needs a Savior; and if we are going to be successful in catching men, we must preach Christ crucified—not His life only but His death. And if we are only faithful in doing this, we shall succeed. And why? Because there is His promise: "If you follow Me, I will make you fishers of men." That promise holds just as good

to you and me as it did to His disciples, and is as true now
as it was in their time.

Think of Paul up yonder. People are going up every day
and every hour, men and women who have been brought to
Christ through his writings. He set streams in motion that
have flowed on for more than a thousand years. I can
imagine men going up there, and saying, "Paul, I thank you
for writing that letter to the Ephesians; I found Christ in
that." "Paul, I thank you for writing that epistle to the
Corinthians." "Paul, I found Christ in that epistle to the
Philippians." "I thank you, Paul, for that epistle to the
Galatians; I found Christ in that." And so, I suppose, they
are going up still, thanking Paul all the while for what he
had done. Ah, when Paul was put in prison he did not fold
his hands and sit down in idleness! No, he began to write;
and his epistles have come down through the long ages of
time, and brought thousands on thousands to a knowledge
of Christ crucified. Yes, Christ said to Paul, "I will make
you a fisher of men if you will follow Me," and he has been
fishing for souls ever since. The devil thought he had done
a very wise thing when he got Paul into prison, but he was
very much mistaken; he overdid it for once. I have no doubt
Paul has thanked God ever since for that Philippian gaol,
and his stripes and imprisonment there. I am sure the world
has made more by it than we shall ever know till we get to
heaven.

5. The "I Will" of Comfort.

The next "I will" is in John, fourteenth chapter, verse
eighteen: "I will not leave you comfortless."

To me it is a sweet thought that Christ has not left us alone in this dark wilderness here below. Although He has gone up on high, and taken His seat by the Father's throne, He has not left us comfortless. The better translation is, "I will not leave you orphans." He did not leave Joseph when they cast him into prison. "God was with him." When Daniel was cast into the den of lions, they had to put the Almighty in with him. They were so bound together that they could not be separated, and so God went down into the den of lions with Daniel.

If we have got Christ with us, we can do all things. Do not let us be thinking how weak we are. Let us lift up our eyes to Him, and think of Him as our Elder Brother, who has all power given to Him in heaven and on earth. He says: "Lo, I am with you alway, even unto the end of the world." Some of our children and friends leave us, and it is a very sad hour. But, thank God, the believer and Christ shall never be separated! He is with us here, and we shall be with Him in person by and by, and shall see Him in His beauty. But not only is He with us, but He has sent us the Holy Ghost. Let us honor the Holy Ghost by acknowledging that He is here in our midst. He has power to give sight to the blind, liberty to the captive, and to open the ears of the deaf that they may hear the glorious words of the Gospel.

6. The "I Will" of Resurrection.

Then there is another I will in John, sixth chapter, verse forty; it occurs four times in the chapter: "I will raise him up at the last day."

I rejoice to think that I have a Savior who has power over death. My blessed Master holds the keys him, and I got more comfort out of that promise "I will raise him up at the last day," than anything else in the Bible. How it cheered me! How it lighted up my path! And as I went into the room and looked upon the lovely face of that brother, how that passage ran through my soul: "Thy brother shall rise again." I said, "Thank God for that promise." It was worth more than the world to me.

When we laid him in the grave, it seemed as if I could hear the voice of Jesus Christ saying, "Thy brother shall rise again." Blessed promise of the resurrection! Blessed "I will!" "I will raise him up at the last day."

7. The "I Will" of Glory.

Now the next I will is in John, seventeenth chapter, twenty-fourth verse: "Father, I will that they also, whom Thou hast given Me, be with Me where I am."

This was in His last prayer in the guest-chamber, on the last night before He was crucified and died that terrible death on Calvary. Many a believer's countenance begins to light up at the thought that he shall see the King in His beauty by and by. Yes; there is a glorious day before us in the future. Some think that on the first day we are converted we have got everything. To be sure, we get salvation for the past and peace for the present; but then there is the glory for the future in store. That's what kept Paul rejoicing. He said, "These light afflictions, these few stripes, these few brickbats and stones that they throw at me—why, the glory that is beyond excels them so much that I count them as nothing, nothing at all, so that I may win Christ." And so, when things go against us, let us cheer up; let us remember that the night will soon pass away, and the morning dawn upon us. Death never comes there. It is banished from that heavenly land. Sickness, and pain, and sorrow, come not there to mar that grand and glorious home where we shall be by and by with the Master. God's family will be all together there. Glorious future, my friends! Yes, glorious day! and it may be a great deal nearer than many of us think. During these few days we are here let us stand steadfast and firm, and by and by we shall be in the unbroken circle in yon world of light, and have the King in our midst.

34458483R00070

Made in the USA
Lexington, KY
23 March 2019